CALIFORNIA
sol food

Library of Congress Number: 2004105355
ISBN 0-9618474-1-7

Edited and Manufactured by Favorite Recipes® Press, an imprint of:

FRP™

P.O. Box 305142
Nashville, Tennessee 37230
800-358-0560

Art director: Steve Newman
Project manager: Tanis Westbrook
Project editor: Debbie Van Mol

Manufactured in the United States of America
First printing: 2004
15,000 copies

CASUAL
COOKING
FROM THE
JUNIOR
LEAGUE
OF SAN DIEGO

CALIFORNIA sol food

FOOD PHOTOGRAPHY BY FRANKIE FRANKENY

CALIFORNIA SOL FOOD

MANAGING EDITORS
Lisa Barnhouse-Gal
Angela Wilson-Gyetvan
Kate Ancell

DESIGN AND EDITING
Kate Ancell

MARKETING AND PR
Suzanne Miller

RECIPE COLLECTION AND TESTING
Tina Bartholomew
Sabrina Parr

SALES
Bobbie Basta

UNDERWRITING
Jacqueline Reed
Arianna Jones

TREASURER
Diane St. John

DEVELOPMENT TEAM
Melissa Abrams, Sharon Amend, Mary Kay Bates, Jennifer Beamer, Alexis Brausa, Jessica Cisneros, Melia Crousore,
Lisa Dearen, Theodora Georggin, Michelle Gierke-Ristad, Melissa Grangaard, Kimberly Howatt, Barbara Kramer,
Kathryn Kulik, Alyssa Lange, Lori Lange, Lynda Levine, Alison Miller, Kristin Mullin, Beth Nelson, Lorrin Ortiz-Mena, Liza Osbun,
LeeAnne Owens, Debbie Rider, Lisa Schroeder, Carolyn Spears, Kristen Spector, Shelly Stephenson-Podlich, Alison Sullivan,
Lisa Thompson, Stephanie Ward, Hallie Waters, Sharon Watkins

FOOD PHOTOGRAPHER
Frankie Frankeny

FOOD STYLIST
Diane Gsell

CREATIVE DIRECTOR
Amanda Vine

acknowledgments

The Junior League of San Diego and *California Sol Food* would like to thank all the League members who contributed their time, talents, and expertise and helped make this book what it is.

HEAD TESTERS

Bonnie Adams, Kate Ancell, Karen Anisko, Lisa Barnhouse-Gal, Tina Bartholomew, Jennifer Beamer, Karen Coakley, Tina Colburn, Mary Ann Del Fiorentino, Cathleen Edwards, Sheryl Gerbracht, Cauleen Glass, Pamela Goldner, Harriet Hall, Brenda Henn, Martha Himelblau, Arianna Jones, Barbara Kramer, Kathryn Kulik, Lori Lange, Lynn Leclercq, Julie MacDonald, Carole Mayo, Jill McDonald, Alison Miller, Kathleen Murrell, Kathryn Nicol, Liza Osbun, Sabrina Parr, Susan Piegza, Anna Pinsoneault, Susan Polizzotto, Elizabeth Ranta, Janet Reardon, Catherine Rogers, Brooke Cameron Scigousky, Emily Shannon, Shannon Stafford Shelton, Kimberly Soltero, Alison Sullivan, Lisa Thompson, Stephanie Ward, Hallie Waters, Leslie Wicker, Loreen Wilhelmy, Angela Wilson-Gyetvan, Erika Wisk, Sharon Worman

PHOTOGRAPHERS

Murray Ancell, Courtney Blackwell, Gemma Doyle, Sally Duff, Margaret Egler, Heather Gioia, Stephanie Hicks, Alison Miller, Beth Nelson, Andrea Schuman, Alice Spacova, Julie Tolby

RECIPE SUBMITTERS

Kate Ancell, Kathleen Baczynksi, Lisa Barnhouse-Gal, Tina Bartholomew, Suzanne Beavers, Dee Benson, Mary Britschgi, Tina Campbell, Jennifer Cavanaugh, Michelle Chambers, Karen Coakley, Judy Courtemanche, Chrysten Cunningham, Mary Ann Del Fiorentino, Michele DeMayo, Cathleen Edwards, Carolyn Elledge, Maureen Farrell, Aimee Lepore Faucett, Jill Faucher, Erika Forbes, Marisa Vallbona Freeman, Sheryl Gerbracht, Heather Gioia, Celeste Greene, Brenda Henn, Martha Himelblau, Diana Holker, Ethel Jordan, Kathleen Kane-Murrell, Kathleen Knotts-Lavine, Barbara Kramer, Kathryn Kulik, Lori Lange, Lisa Linquest, Julie MacDonald, Carole Mayo, Gloria McCoy, Sandra Melchior, Alison Miller, Mary Mims, Erin Moran, Beth Nelson, Kathryn Nicol, Liza Osbun, Anne Otterson, Sabrina Parr, Christiana Payne, Susan Piegza, Kimberly Baker Potter, Beth Ranlett, Elizabeth Ranta, Carolyn Rentto, Catherine Rogers, Brooke Cameron Scigousky, Shannon Stafford Shelton, Carolyn Spears, Lydia Stacy, Alison Sullivan, Terre Sychterz, Lisa Thompson, Betty Ward, Stephanie Ward, Hallie Waters, Misty Westbrook, Loreen Wilhelmy, Sharon Worman, Carolyn Yorston

introduction

Greetings from the Junior League of San Diego! We are thrilled that you are joining us as we celebrate 75 years of commitment to our community. We hope you will take a moment to learn a little about who we are and what we do...

In 1927, a young San Diego woman named Lillian Bradley met both the director and the president of the Junior League of Pasadena. She was so inspired by the work they were doing in their community that she returned home determined to establish a League of her own in San Diego. She didn't waste any time; later that year, with her friend Emily Clayton, Lillian Bradley started the ball rolling by founding the Junior Committee for San Diego Charities. Two years later, in 1929, the Junior Committee for San Diego Charities was accepted as a member of the Association of Junior Leagues International (AJLI), making the Junior League of San Diego the fifth League in the state of California and the 105th League overall to join the AJLI.

Since the day of our inception 75 years ago, we have accomplished many great things, from our first project—establishing a day nursery for the children of working parents—to providing assistance to hospitals and museums; advocating for victims of domestic violence and juvenile justice; establishing programs for seniors; and promoting community leadership throughout San Diego.

Our current focus at JLSD is education; we are committed to ensuring that each and every child is given the basic necessities for receiving a quality education. Through programs such as Changes through Children, in which San Diego's youth learn the value of community service, and Libraries Now, in which League members construct mini-libraries for all new elementary school teachers, the Junior League of San Diego has made an enormous impact in the community. Other projects include Storefront, a shelter dedicated to assisting San Diego's homeless teen population, and Education Toolbox, which provides every first grader in 19 elementary schools with a "toolbox" containing a backpack, a video of tips for math and verbal skill improvement, and school supplies. The Junior League of San Diego realizes that the key to lifelong education is a love of learning, and to that end, we are committed to fostering programs that develop a child's imagination, curiosity, and confidence.

Junior League of San Diego members contribute over 60,000 volunteer hours and raise more than $150,000 per year for our community assistance programs through endowments, grants, and special events. This year, we are proud to launch our newest fund-raiser, *California Sol Food: Casual Cooking from the Junior League of San Diego*, celebrating our Southern California lifestyle with simple, yet refreshing recipes that reflect our warm, sunny climate. Filled with everything from scrumptious seafood dishes to savory salads, delectable desserts to mouth-watering midnight snacks, *California Sol Food* encompasses everything there is to taste and to toast in our magnificent city. Enjoy!

sponsors

California Sol Food would like to thank all those whose kind donations helped make this book a reality. We could not have done it without your support.

Mary Kay Burns-Blue, Libby Carson, Jeanne Frost, Kathryn Gambill, Marcia Beck Griggs, Amy Jackson, Liz Jessop, Minerva Kunzel, Perry Ann Kurtz, Paula Landale, Alyssa Lange, Emily McCutchan, Erika Otto, Qualcomm Employee Matching Gift Fund, Ruth Whitney Robinson, Audrey Rohde, The San Diego Foundation's Kathryn B. And Daniel L. Sullivan Family Fund, Sheryl and Bob Scarano, Sylvia Sherwood, Maxine Underwood, Ginger Wallace, Betty Jo Williams, Gayle Wilson

The 2003-04 Junior League of San Diego Board of Directors
Christie Thoene, President; Lisa Linquest, Vice President; Pamela Bumann, Treasurer; Julie Tolby, Recording Secretary; Caroline Wohl, Communications Director; Margaret Egler, Community Director; Misty Westbrook, Fund Development Director; Stephanie McGuire, Membership Director; Erika Otto, President-Elect; Martha Shumaker, Sustainer Advisor; Ruth Bush, Sr. SPAC; Kerry Walker, Nominating; Carmel Deetman, Board Assistant

AND A VERY SPECIAL THANKS TO:
Steven and Lisa Gal
Donna Hine Daniels
In loving memory of Dorothy Sylvester Hine, member of the Junior Leagues of Kansas City, Missouri, and St. Louis, Missouri, 1935-2003, by her daughter, Donna Hine Daniels, member of the Junior Leagues of Kansas City, Missouri, and San Diego, California.
Jane Trevor Fetter

contents

Morning is a special time of day for those of us making our lives here at the edge of the Pacific.

breakfast

Morning is a special time of day for those of us making our lives here at the edge of the Pacific. As the rising sun drills a hole through the misty marine layer swirling over San Elijo Lagoon, joggers start to pound the boardwalk in Pacific Beach, while surfers from 16 to 60 congregate at 15th Street, looking for the best swell. The horses in Del Mar are up too, ready for the day's races to come. And in East County, the mountaintops glow with the first rays of the dawn's early light as the desert flowers start to open up.

The morning hour is a rare time of peace and harmony for us early risers, before life's alarm goes off and we're running to beat the clock, the rush-hour traffic, and the kids' school bell. With all these commitments, who has time to strap on an apron and prepare a feast served on fine linen and matching flatware? No one we know.

But that doesn't mean that we don't want to feed ourselves, our families, and our ever-present visitors good, nourishing, delicious food. So, we've decided that we can have it all—within reason, of course. Weekdays may mean a grab-and-go meal of our make-ahead, keep-forever granola with a side of fresh strawberries from a roadside stand (can anything beat the smell of a flat of berries picked just that morning?), but we do like to raise the bar on the weekends. How great is it to sit down to a table of Huevos Rancheros, Fruit Salad with Lime Syrup (take the compliments; hide this cookbook), and a plate of warm muffins?

So, fuel up, grab your yoga mat, and hit the local coffeehouse feeling virtuous; or take a leisurely post-breakfast stroll down to the Children's Pool in La Jolla to watch the seals come out to sunbathe. However you want to play it, it's your day.

egg scramble with sun-dried tomatoes

The easiest way to make them eat their veggies—and ask for more.

3   garlic cloves, minced
1   tablespoon extra-virgin olive oil
2   cups chopped broccoli
1   cup sliced cremini mushrooms
1/3 cup sliced sun-dried tomatoes
3   eggs
3   egg whites
1/3 cup nonfat, 1% or 2% milk
    Salt and pepper to taste
    Crumbled goat cheese to taste

TIP   *Make this nutritious meal even better by substituting egg whites for the whole eggs.*

Coat a large skillet with olive oil nonstick cooking spray and heat over medium heat. Sauté the garlic in the olive oil in the hot skillet for 1 minute. Stir in the broccoli, mushrooms and sun-dried tomatoes. Sauté for 2 minutes longer. Reduce the heat to medium-low. Cook, covered, for 2 minutes or until the broccoli is tender-crisp, stirring occasionally. Remove the sautéed vegetables to a bowl.

Whisk the eggs, egg whites, nonfat milk, salt and pepper in a bowl until blended. Scramble the eggs in a nonstick skillet over medium-high heat. Stir in the broccoli mixture. Spoon the egg mixture into individual bowls and sprinkle with goat cheese. Serve immediately.

Serves 2

creamy scrambled eggs

A decadent start to a lazy Saturday morning—hit the waves later and burn off the calories surfing.

10   eggs
     Salt and pepper to taste
2   tablespoons butter, or nonstick
     cooking spray
3   ounces cream cheese, cubed
1/3 cup chopped fresh chives
     Chopped fresh parsley
     (optional)

TIP   *For scrambled eggs that are super-light and fluffy, add a little water while you whisk them.*

Whisk the eggs, salt and pepper in a bowl until blended. Melt the butter in a large skillet over low heat. Pour the egg mixture into the skillet, tilting the pan to ensure even coverage. Cook over low heat just until the eggs begin to set, lifting the edge with a spatula to allow the uncooked eggs to flow underneath. Add the cream cheese to the eggs.

Cook until the eggs are the desired degree of doneness and the cream cheese melts, stirring gently. Sprinkle with the chives and parsley. Serve immediately.

Serves 4 to 5

huevos rancheros

Serve with a side of warm tortillas and pass the Tabasco sauce.

RANCHERO SAUCE

1	large onion, chopped
1	large green bell pepper, chopped
3	garlic cloves, crushed
1	teaspoon salt
3	tablespoons olive oil
3	tablespoons flour
2	teaspoons chili powder
1	teaspoon cumin
1	teaspoon sugar (optional)
1/2	teaspoon coarsely ground pepper
2	pounds fresh tomatoes, seeded and crushed, or 2 (15-ounce) cans crushed tomatoes, drained

EGGS AND ASSEMBLY

1	dozen eggs
8	ounces Monterey Jack cheese, shredded

TIP *Minimize early-morning labor by preparing the night before and refrigerating. Add an additional ten minutes to the baking time if baked cold. Freezes beautifully.*

RANCHERO SAUCE   Cook the onion, bell pepper, garlic and salt in the olive oil in a skillet until the vegetables are brown, stirring frequently. Stir in the flour, chili powder, cumin, sugar and pepper. Add the tomatoes and mix well. Simmer for 15 minutes, stirring occasionally.

EGGS   Preheat the oven to 350 degrees. Whisk the eggs in a bowl until blended. Lightly scramble the eggs in a nonstick skillet and spoon into a lightly greased 9×13-inch baking dish. Spoon the sauce over the eggs and sprinkle with the cheese. Bake for 25 minutes.

Serves 8

huevos rancheros

mexican eggs

Garnish with a cilantro leaf and serve with the great Guacamole on page 116.

9 ounces Monterey Jack cheese, shredded

9 ounces sharp Cheddar cheese, shredded

1 cup sour cream

1 (4-ounce) can green chiles, chopped

6 eggs, lightly beaten

Preheat the oven to 350 degrees. Combine the Monterey Jack cheese, Cheddar cheese, sour cream, green chiles and eggs in a bowl and stir until mixed. Spoon the egg mixture into a 9×13-inch baking dish. Bake for 30 to 40 minutes or until set.

Serves 6 to 8

crème brûlée french toast

Rich and delicious. To really indulge, serve with a bubbly mimosa on the side.

1	cup packed brown sugar
1/2	cup (1 stick) unsalted butter
2	tablespoons corn syrup
1	loaf French toast bread or challah, sliced and crusts trimmed
1 1/2	cups half-and-half
5	eggs
1	teaspoon vanilla extract
1	teaspoon Grand Marnier
1/4	teaspoon salt

Heat the brown sugar, butter and corn syrup in a heavy saucepan over medium heat until blended, stirring frequently. Pour the syrup into a 9×13-inch baking dish, tilting the dish to ensure even coverage. Arrange the bread slices in a single layer over the syrup.

Whisk the half-and-half, eggs, vanilla, liqueur and salt in a bowl until blended. Pour over the prepared layers. Chill, covered, for 8 to 24 hours.

Preheat the oven to 350 degrees. Let the bread stand until room temperature. Bake on the middle oven rack for 35 to 40 minutes or until the edges are golden brown and puffed. Garnish each serving with a sprig of mint. Serve with fresh berries.

Serves 6

ham and spinach puff pancake

Elegant and delicious. . .a real showstopper.

PANCAKE
- 1/4 cup (1/2 stick) butter
- 3/4 cup milk
- 2/3 cup flour
- 2 eggs
- 1/2 teaspoon salt

FILLING
- 1 (10-ounce) package frozen chopped spinach, thawed and drained
- 3 tablespoons butter
- 2 cups sliced fresh mushrooms
- 1/2 cup chopped onion
- 8 ounces cooked ham, cubed
- 1 1/2 cups (6 ounces) shredded Cheddar cheese

TIP   *This dish is equally delectable with turkey ham and reduced-fat Cheddar cheese.*

PANCAKE   Preheat the oven to 400 degrees. Heat the butter in a 9-inch baking dish in the oven for 2 to 4 minutes or until melted. Whisk the milk, flour, eggs and salt in a bowl for 2 to 3 minutes or until smooth. Pour the batter into the prepared dish. Bake for 20 to 25 minutes or until brown.

FILLING   Squeeze the excess moisture from the spinach. Melt the butter in a 10-inch skillet. Add the mushrooms and onion to the butter and cook over medium heat for 5 to 7 minutes or until the mushrooms are tender, stirring occasionally. Stir in the spinach and ham.

Cook for 3 to 4 minutes longer or until the filling is heated through, stirring occasionally. Stir in 1 cup of the cheese. Spoon the spinach mixture into the center of the hot pancake and sprinkle with the remaining 1/2 cup cheese. Cut into wedges and serve immediately.

Serves 6

cinnamon nut ring

Delicious straight up, and heavenly when garnished with fresh strawberries and whipped cream.

3 cups flour
2 teaspoons baking powder
2 teaspoons cinnamon
1/2 teaspoon salt
2 cups sugar
1 cup shortening
1/4 teaspoon almond extract
1/4 teaspoon vanilla extract
4 eggs, at room temperature
1 cup milk
1 cup chopped walnuts

TIP *To release the cake from the pan, you may need to run a small metal spatula around the edge of the cake.*

Preheat the oven to 350 degrees. Sift the flour, baking powder, cinnamon and salt together. Beat the sugar and shortening in a mixing bowl until creamy, scraping the bowl occasionally. Beat in the flavorings. Add the eggs 1 at a time, beating well after each addition. Add the milk and flour mixture alternately, beginning and ending with the milk and beating at low speed just until the ingredients are blended. Fold in the walnuts.

Spoon the batter into a greased and floured angel food cake pan. Bake for 75 to 80 minutes or until a wooden pick inserted halfway between the tube and the outer edge of the cake pan comes out clean. Cool in the pan for 10 minutes. Invert onto a cake plate, removing the outer rim and leaving the tube in the cake for 20 to 30 minutes longer. Remove the tube and cut into slices. Garnish each serving with whipped cream and sliced fresh fruit. You may substitute a mixture of 1/2 cup chopped walnuts, 1/2 cup chopped almonds and 1/2 teaspoon almond extract for the 1 cup chopped walnuts and 1/4 teaspoon vanilla.

Serves 12 to 16

Fresh berries should be dry, firm, and well-shaped. Eat within a week of purchase. If you cannot eat them that soon, remember that berries freeze well. If buying frozen berries, avoid containers with juice stains. Store fresh berries in their original container, or arrange in a shallow dish lined with paper towels; do not rinse before storing. Top with a paper towel to absorb moisture, and then cover tightly with plastic wrap.

raspberry muffins

A family favorite-by-the-sea.

1	cup packed brown sugar
1 1/2	cups flour
1/4	cup (1/2 stick) butter
1/2	teaspoon cinnamon
1/2	cup whole wheat flour
2	teaspoons baking powder
1	teaspoon cinnamon
1/4	teaspoon salt
1/4	cup sugar
1/4	cup packed brown sugar
1/2	cup (about) milk
1/2	cup (1 stick) butter, softened
1	egg, lightly beaten
1	cup fresh or drained frozen raspberries

Pulse 1 cup brown sugar, 1/2 cup of the all-purpose flour, 1/4 cup butter and 1/2 teaspoon cinnamon in a food processor until crumbly.

Preheat the oven to 400 degrees. Combine the remaining all-purpose flour, whole wheat flour, baking powder, 1 teaspoon cinnamon and salt in a bowl and mix well. Stir in the sugar and 1/4 cup brown sugar. Add the milk, 1/2 cup butter and egg to the flour mixture and stir just until moistened. Fold in the raspberries.

Spoon the batter into paper-lined muffin cups and sprinkle with the streusel topping. Bake for 15 to 20 minutes or until a wooden pick inserted in the centers comes out clean.

Makes 1 dozen muffins

totally berry orange oat muffins

Never has virtue tasted so good—even children will love these.

1/2 cup rolled oats
1/2 cup lowfat buttermilk
1 1/2 cups whole wheat flour
1 teaspoon baking powder
1/2 teaspoon baking soda
1/2 teaspoon cinnamon
1 orange
1/2 cup sugar
1/4 cup canola oil
1 egg
1 cup fresh blueberries
1/2 cup dried cranberries
(optional)

Preheat the oven to 400 degrees. Combine the oats and buttermilk in a bowl and mix well. Mix the whole wheat flour, baking powder, baking soda and cinnamon together. Grate the zest from the orange into a bowl. Squeeze enough juice from the grated orange to measure 1/2 cup and add to the orange zest.

Whisk the sugar, canola oil and egg into the orange juice mixture until mixed. Stir in the oats mixture. Add the flour mixture and mix just until moistened. Fold in the blueberries and cranberries. Spoon the batter into muffin cups sprayed with nonstick cooking spray. Bake for 15 minutes or until the muffins test done.

Makes 1 dozen muffins

cranberry orange bread

Fantastic around the holiday season and a great "gift" bread.

2 cups flour
1 1/2 teaspoons baking powder
1 teaspoon salt
1/2 teaspoon baking soda
1 cup sugar
3/4 cup water
1/3 cup fresh orange juice
2 tablespoons vegetable oil
1 egg
1 tablespoon grated orange zest
1 cup chopped nuts (optional)
1 cup fresh or unthawed frozen
cranberry halves

Preheat the oven to 350 degrees. Grease the bottom of a 5×9-inch loaf pan. Mix the flour, baking powder, salt and baking soda together.

Combine the sugar, water, orange juice, oil, egg and orange zest in a bowl and mix well. Add the dry ingredients to the orange mixture and stir just until moistened. Fold in the nuts and cranberries. Spoon the batter into the prepared loaf pan.

Bake for 50 to 60 minutes or until a wooden pick inserted in the center comes out clean. Cool in the pan for 10 minutes. Remove to a wire rack to cool completely. Store, tightly wrapped, in the refrigerator.

Makes 1 loaf

peach breakfast cake

Great for a family breakfast and charming for guests.

SOUR CREAM TOPPING

1	cup sour cream
1/4	cup sugar
1	egg white, lightly beaten
1/4	teaspoon almond extract

CAKE

1/2	cup (1 stick) butter
1/2	cup sugar
1	teaspoon grated orange zest
1/4	teaspoon almond extract
2	eggs
3/4	cup flour
3	ripe firm large peaches, peeled and cut into halves
	Cinnamon and sugar to taste

TIP *Those of us who are all thumbs when it comes to peeling delicate fruit will be happy to know that canned peaches work just as well in this recipe.*

TOPPING Combine the sour cream, sugar, egg white and flavoring in a bowl and mix well.

CAKE Preheat the oven to 350 degrees. Beat the butter, 1/2 cup sugar, orange zest and flavoring in a mixing bowl until combined. Add the eggs 1 at a time, beating well after each addition. Add the flour and beat until blended.

Spoon the batter into a buttered and floured 9-inch springform pan with removable bottom. Arrange the peach halves cut side down over the batter. Bake for 25 to 30 minutes or until the cake just begins to pull from the side of the pan and is light brown in color. Remove the cake from the oven and spoon the topping around the peaches.

Bake for 10 minutes longer. Cool in the pan on a wire rack for 30 minutes. Run a sharp knife around the edge of the cake and remove the rim. Place the cake on a platter and sprinkle lightly with cinnamon and sugar to taste. Serve warm or at room temperature. You may prepare in advance and let stand at room temperature for up to 3 hours or chill, covered, for up to 8 hours.

Serves 8 to 9

peach breakfast cake

homemade applesauce

Don't let the simplicity fool you—this is always a hit.

12 Golden Delicious apples,
    peeled and thinly sliced
1/2 cup water
1/4 cup sugar
1/4 cup packed brown sugar
1 tablespoon lemon juice
1 teaspoon (or more) cinnamon
1/2 teaspoon allspice

Combine the apples, water, sugar, brown sugar, lemon juice, cinnamon and allspice in a large saucepan and mix well. Cook, covered, over medium-low heat for 3 to 4 hours or until the desired consistency, stirring occasionally. Serve warm or chilled.

Serves 6 to 8

fruit salad with lime syrup

The ultimate fruit salad with a modern twist.

LIME SYRUP
1/2 cup fresh lime juice
    (about 4 limes)
1/2 cup water
1/4 cup sugar

SALAD
1 (2-pound) watermelon, cut into
    1-inch cubes
2 nectarines, cut into wedges
1/2 small cantaloupe, cut into
    thin wedges
1/2 small honeydew melon, cut into
    thin wedges
1/2 (24-ounce) jar pink grapefruit
    sections, drained
    Grated zest of 1 lime

SYRUP   Combine the lime juice, water and sugar in a small saucepan and mix well. Simmer for 10 minutes or until slightly thickened, stirring occasionally. Let stand until cool. The syrup may be prepared up to 1 week in advance.

SALAD   Combine the watermelon, nectarines, cantaloupe, honeydew melon, grapefruit and lime zest in a large bowl. Add the syrup and toss gently to coat.

Serves 8

granola

A traditional morning dish from the Land of Fruits and Nuts.

1 pound old-fashioned rolled oats
1 cup blanched sliced almonds
3/4 cup whole cashews
1/2 cup packed brown sugar
1 tablespoon grated orange zest
1 teaspoon cinnamon
1/2 teaspoon grated fresh nutmeg
1/2 cup (1 stick) unsalted butter, cubed
1/3 cup maple syrup
1 cup shredded coconut, toasted
1 cup coarsely chopped dried fruit (raisins, dates, figs and/or apricots)

TIP   *To toast coconut, spread the shreds on a baking sheet. Toast for 10 minutes while the granola is in the oven. Serve with yogurt and fresh fruit.*

Preheat the oven to 325 degrees. Spray two 9×13-inch baking pans with nonstick cooking spray. Combine the oats, almonds, cashews, brown sugar, orange zest, cinnamon and nutmeg in a mixing bowl. Beat at low speed for 1 minute.

Heat the butter and syrup in a saucepan until blended, stirring occasionally. Add the syrup mixture to the oats mixture and mix just until moistened. Spread the oat mixture in 1 of the prepared baking pans and pat lightly.

Bake for 25 minutes. Invert the mixture into the remaining prepared pan and pat lightly. Bake for 20 to 25 minutes longer or until the granola is golden brown. Let stand until cool. Break the granola into bite-size pieces and mix with the coconut and dried fruit in a bowl. Store in an airtight container for up to 1 week.

Makes 20 (1/2-cup) servings

The best brunches offer great food served with a bit of drama.

brunch

There's just something special about brunch. We like to get out and experience all the great things our fabulous town has to offer, and dining al fresco in the mid-morning is the perfect gateway to a long, leisurely afternoon spent having fun with friends and family. We also love both the friendly don't-bother-with-your-hair-if-you-don't-want-to feel of a casual occasion and the appeal of its opposite—the chance to get out the stem crystal and silver servers at 10:30 am if the mood strikes. Offering something for every taste and lifestyle, a brunch is easily the most versatile way to entertain—and that's what we like most about it.

The key? Start things off right with a pitcher of something fun and fruity, be it our Fresh Mango Smoothies for the younger crowd (guaranteed to give kids an energy spike that you may or may not thank us for later) or the more adults-only Rancho Santa Fe Spritzer. With your friends settled in, and unconcerned about getting sand in the French toast, it's time to set out the long table. To us, brunch means buffet—lots of delicious, healthy food that people can pile on anything from fine china to paper plates—preferably with abandon. And don't forget the cardinal rule: location, location, location. (One in-the-know showstopper venue to impress out-of-towners is in South County— head down to Otay Lake Reservoir—don't forget your fishing poles!—and watch the rowers work out at the Olympic Training Center while you sit idly by in the cool shade.)

The best brunches offer great food served with a bit of drama. We love touches like big beautiful bouquets of fresh flowers bought that morning at the Farmer's Market or a centerpiece of freshly cooked tortilla chips served in a sombrero from Tijuana.

However you like to entertain, whether it's outside on the patio with the sounds of waves and gulls as your background music or inside with a string quartet and fine linens, this is a fabulous time of day to do it. So, dig out that espresso machine, dust off your patio umbrella, and get started with your guest list. We know you'll have a great time.

brunch menus

spring baby shower
citrus salad
crustless crab quiche
asparagus with red
pepper confetti (Dinner, p. 139)
pineapple meringue
cake (Dessert, p. 180)

This pretty menu is perfect for a joyous celebration. We think it's
a fun idea to serve this cake, decorated with one blue and one
pink candle on top, after the presents have been opened—tell all
the guests to make a wish and blow for good luck!

summer celebration
rancho santa fe spritzer
heirloom tomato salad with tapenade and
chèvre toasts (Dinner, p. 137)
summer frittata
strawberry shortcake (Dessert, p. 186)

This is a wonderful menu to serve at a brunch honoring a visiting guest. The signature California fruits and vegetables are fresh and delicious, and beautiful when displayed on pretty pewter or china dishes.

harvest brunch
baby greens tossed with strawberry vinaigrette (Lunch, p. 72)
french toast with orange syrup
golden harvest muffins
iced chunky pumpkin cookies (Midnight Snack, p. 205)

The perfect back-to-school brunch. We love to celebrate the change in seasons (even if the weather's not cooperating) by serving this traditional menu with a twist. Why not try it out at your first fall committee meeting or pre-football game get-together?

holiday gathering
pumpkin chile soup (Lunch, p. 55)
avocado salad (Lunch, p. 58)
lobster quiche
gingerbread cake

We've found that pairing spicy soup with a cool green salad is unexpected, fresh, and effective. The lobster adds an elegant touch to this festive menu, and absolutely everyone feels merry and bright about our Gingerbread Cake.

rancho santa fe spritzer

Fresh, zingy, and delicious. Great for a pre-race pick-me-up.

2	cups fresh strawberries and fresh raspberries
2	cups apricot nectar, chilled
2	cups seltzer, chilled
2	cups ginger ale, chilled
2	cups white grape juice, chilled
1 1/2	cups vodka (optional)

Spread the strawberries and raspberries in a single layer on a baking sheet. Freeze for 8 to 10 hours. Remove the berries to a resealable plastic freezer bag and store in the freezer.

Combine the apricot nectar, seltzer, ginger ale, grape juice and vodka in a large pitcher or punch bowl and mix well. Add the frozen berries just before serving and pour into glasses or ladle into punch cups.

Makes 8 (1-cup) servings

fresh mango smoothie

Garnish with a sprig of mint and a lemon slice—so fresh and sweet.

1	large or 2 small mangoes, peeled and cut into chunks
1	cup plain nonfat yogurt
2	tablespoons sugar
1	teaspoon fresh lemon juice
1/2	cup ice water
3	(or more) ice cubes

Process the mangoes in a blender until puréed. Combine 1 cup of the purée, the yogurt, sugar and lemon juice in a blender and process until smooth. Add the ice water and process until combined. Add the ice cubes and process just until the ice is crushed, adding additional ice cubes if needed for the desired consistency. Pour the smoothie into frosted glasses. Garnish and serve immediately.

Serves 2

italian frittata with goat cheese

A Sunday brunch staple, and the ideal main dish for a family meal.

2¹/2 tablespoons unsalted butter

¹/3 cup minced onion

¹/3 cup minced green bell pepper

5   eggs

3   egg whites

5   or 6 slices prosciutto, cut into bite-size pieces

1   (7-ounce) can artichoke hearts, drained and coarsely chopped

¹/2 cup chopped fresh basil

¹/2 cup chopped cooked potatoes (2 or 3 small red bliss potatoes or 1 Yukon Gold potato)

¹/2 teaspoon salt
    Ground pepper to taste

2   ounces goat cheese, crumbled

TIP   *Did you know that it is easier to separate eggs when the eggs are cold? This frittata is unbelievable when served with fresh orange juice, hot coffee, and a side of sourdough toast.*

Heat the butter in a large cast-iron skillet over medium heat. Add the onion and bell pepper and mix well. Cook for 8 minutes or until the vegetables are tender but not brown, stirring frequently.

Preheat the broiler. Whisk the eggs and egg whites in a bowl until blended. Stir in the prosciutto, artichokes, basil, potatoes, salt and pepper. Pour the egg mixture over the onion mixture, tilting the skillet to ensure even coverage. Sprinkle the cheese over the top.

Cook over medium-low heat for 10 to 15 minutes or until the center is almost set; do not stir. Broil for 5 minutes or until brown. Cut into wedges and serve immediately.

Serves 4 to 6

summer frittata

Spicy, cheesy, and bursting with vegetables. What's not to like?

4   to 5 ounces sweet Italian
       sausage
10   to 11 ounces hot Italian
       sausage
1   dozen eggs
$1/2$ teaspoon salt
$1/8$ teaspoon pepper
$11/4$ cups (5 ounces) shredded sharp
       Cheddar cheese
2   tablespoons unsalted butter
1   tablespoon olive oil
2   shallots, finely chopped
8   ounces fresh mushrooms,
       thinly sliced
2   small zucchini, thinly sliced
1   garlic clove, minced
$1/4$ teaspoon salt
$1/8$ teaspoon pepper
3   Roma tomatoes, sliced
$1/4$ cup (1 ounce) shredded sharp
       Cheddar cheese

Cook the sausage in a skillet over medium heat for 10 minutes or until brown, turning occasionally; drain. Cool and cut into $1/4$-inch slices. Preheat the oven to 425 degrees.

Whisk the eggs, $1/2$ teaspoon salt and $1/8$ teaspoon pepper in a bowl until blended. Stir in $11/4$ cups cheese. Heat the butter and olive oil in an ovenproof skillet over medium-high heat. Sauté the shallots in the butter mixture for 3 minutes or until tender but not brown. Add the mushrooms and sauté for 1 to 2 minutes. Stir in the zucchini and sauté for 2 minutes. Add the garlic and sauté for 1 minute longer. Arrange the sliced sausage around the vegetables and sprinkle with $1/4$ teaspoon salt and $1/8$ teaspoon pepper.

Pour the egg mixture evenly over the sausage and vegetables. Cook over medium-low heat for 5 minutes or until almost set, stirring occasionally. Arrange the tomatoes around the edge of the skillet and sprinkle $1/4$ cup cheese over the top. Bake for 10 to 15 minutes or until puffed and brown.

Invert the frittata onto a plate and invert again onto a serving platter. Garnish with dollops of sour cream and julienned fresh basil. Cut into wedges. Serve warm or at room temperature.

Serves 4 to 6

summer frittata

veggie pattie-cakes

A kid-favorite treat that grown-ups will also enjoy.

EGG PATTIES

1/2	cup plain bread crumbs
1/2	cup (2 ounces) grated Parmesan cheese
1/2	cup chopped fresh cilantro
1	garlic clove, minced
6	eggs, beaten
1	(6-ounce) can chopped black olives, drained
2	tablespoons chopped fresh chives
2	tablespoons drained capers Salt and pepper to taste
1/4	cup olive oil

TOMATO SAUCE

1	small onion, finely chopped
1	garlic clove, minced
2	tablespoons olive oil
1	(14-ounce) can diced tomatoes
1	teaspoon sugar
1/2	cup water
3	tablespoons chopped fresh basil

PATTIES   Combine the bread crumbs, cheese, cilantro and garlic in a bowl and mix well. Stir in the eggs, olives, chives, capers, salt and pepper. Heat the olive oil in a skillet until hot but not smoking. Drop the egg mixture by rounded tablespoons in batches into the hot oil. Cook for 2 minutes per side or until brown and puffed, adding additional oil as needed. Drain on paper towels.

SAUCE   Sauté the onion and garlic in the olive oil in a skillet until the onion is tender. Stir in the undrained tomatoes and sugar. Simmer for 10 minutes, stirring occasionally. Add the patties to the sauce and simmer for 10 minutes, stirring occasionally. Stir in the water and basil and simmer just until heated through.

Serves 6 to 8

crustless crab quiche

A great brunch dish. . .elegant and satisfying.

12 ounces fresh mushrooms, sliced
2 tablespoons butter
6 eggs
1 cup sour cream
1 cup small curd cottage cheese
1/2 cup (2 ounces) grated
   Parmesan cheese
1/4 cup flour
1 1/4 teaspoons onion powder
1/4 teaspoon salt
1/4 to 1/2 teaspoon Tabasco sauce
2 1/2 cups (10 ounces) shredded
   Monterey Jack cheese
6 to 8 ounces fresh Dungeness
   crab meat, drained and shells
   removed

TIP   *This is a wonderful addition to a buffet table, and it is manna for seafood lovers.*

Preheat the oven to 350 degrees. Sauté the mushrooms in the butter in a skillet until tender; drain. Combine the eggs, sour cream, cottage cheese, Parmesan cheese, flour, onion powder, salt and Tabasco sauce in a food processor fitted with a metal blade and process until blended.

Combine the egg mixture, mushrooms, Monterey Jack cheese and crab meat in a bowl and mix well. Pour the egg mixture into a 9- or 10-inch porcelain quiche dish.

Bake for 45 minutes or until brown and puffy and a knife inserted in the center comes out clean. Let stand for 5 minutes before cutting into wedges.

Serves 8

lobster quiche

This is affordable luxury and will make family and guests feel chic and beloved.

8	ounces cremini mushrooms, stems removed and cut into 1/4-inch slices
1	cup small broccoli florets
1	tablespoon minced onion
1	tablespoon butter
1	cup milk
1	cup light cream
3	eggs, beaten
1	pound cooked lobster, drained and chopped
1/2	teaspoon dry mustard
1/4	teaspoon basil
	Salt and freshly ground pepper to taste
1	unbaked (9-inch) pie shell

TIP   *As an alternative, serve with a tossed green salad for a light summer dinner.*

Preheat the oven to 450 degrees. Sauté the mushrooms, broccoli and onion in the butter in a skillet until the onion is tender and the vegetables have released their liquid; drain. Whisk the milk, light cream and eggs in a bowl until blended. Stir in the lobster and sautéed vegetables. Add the dry mustard, basil, salt and pepper and mix well.

Pour the lobster mixture into the pie shell. Bake for 10 minutes. Reduce the oven temperature to 325 degrees and bake for 20 to 30 minutes longer or just until the center is firm.

Serves 6 to 8

lobster quiche

new quiche lorraine

Real men do eat quiche—especially this one.

8	slices Canadian bacon, cut into $1/4 \times 1$-inch strips
1	tablespoon butter
1	leek with top, cut diagonally into $1/4$-inch slices
4	eggs
1	cup half-and-half
$1/4$	teaspoon salt
$1/4$	teaspoon freshly ground pepper
6	ounces Gruyère or Jarlsberg cheese, shredded
$1 1/2$	teaspoons cornstarch
1	Quiche Pastry, baked (page 39)

Preheat the oven to 325 degrees.

Sauté the bacon in a nonstick skillet over medium heat for 2 to 3 minutes or just until the bacon begins to brown. Remove the bacon to a paper towel to drain. Drain the skillet and add the butter. Sauté the leek in the butter over medium-low heat for 10 minutes or until tender.

Whisk the eggs in a bowl until frothy. Stir in the half-and-half, salt and pepper. Toss the cheese with the cornstarch in a bowl. Add the bacon, leek and cheese mixture to the eggs and mix well. Pour into the pastry shell. Bake for 35 to 40 minutes or until a knife inserted in the center comes out clean, covering the pastry edge with foil to prevent overbrowning if needed. Cool on a wire rack for 15 minutes. Remove the side of the tart pan and place the quiche on a serving platter. Serve warm.

Serves 4 to 6

quiche pastry

1¹/2 cups flour
1/2 teaspoon salt
1/2 cup (1 stick) unsalted butter,
     chilled and cut into small pieces
3   to 4 tablespoons cold water

TIP *To prevent shrinkage, chill
the pastry for about fifteen minutes
before baking.*

Preheat the oven to 425 degrees. Combine the flour and salt in a food processor and process just until mixed. Add the butter and pulse until crumbly. Sprinkle the water over the crumb mixture and pulse until the dough forms a ball.

Roll the dough into a 12-inch round on a lightly floured surface. Drape the round over a rolling pin and carefully transfer to a 9-inch tart pan with a removable bottom. Fit the pastry over the bottom and up the side of the tart pan and trim the edge. Prick the pastry with a fork. Form a double-thick 12-inch square of foil and poke with a few holes. Press the foil into the pastry-lined pan. Bake for 8 minutes and remove the foil. Bake for 4 minutes longer or until the pastry looks dry but not brown. Remove from the oven.

Makes 1 quiche pastry

cheese soufflé

So rich and delicious. Perfect for a ladies' luncheon.

10	slices white bread
	Butter, softened
1	pound extra-sharp Cheddar cheese, shredded
2 1/2	cups milk
8	eggs
1/2	teaspoon white pepper
1	can lobster bisque
1	cup heavy cream

Spread both sides of the bread slices with butter and trim the crusts. Stack the bread slices and cut into quarters. Layer 1/2 of the bread quarters in a single layer in a baking dish. Sprinkle with 1/2 of the cheese. Top with the remaining bread quarters and sprinkle with the remaining cheese.

Whisk the milk, eggs and white pepper in a bowl until blended. Pour the egg mixture over the prepared layers. Chill, covered, for 8 to 10 hours; remove the cover.

Preheat the oven to 325 degrees. Bake for 1 hour. Combine the bisque and heavy cream in a saucepan and mix well. Cook over low heat until thickened, stirring occasionally. Drizzle a small portion of the sauce over the soufflé and serve the remaining sauce on the side.

Serves 10 to 12

crunchy cornmeal and tomato galette

Elegantly delicious. A perfect combination of Indian Summer flavors.

1 cup flour
1/4 cup yellow cornmeal
1/2 cup (1 stick) unsalted butter,
  cut into 1/2-inch pieces
  Coarse salt to taste
1/3 cup ice water
3 tablespoons sour cream
1 teaspoon lemon juice
3 cups (12 ounces) (or more)
  shredded mozzarella cheese
  (not bufala)
3 cups (12 ounces) shredded
  fontina cheese
1/4 cup julienned fresh basil
3 firm ripe Roma tomatoes,
  thinly sliced
  Freshly ground pepper to taste

Freeze the flour, cornmeal and butter for 1 hour. Place the flour, cornmeal and salt on a hard work surface. Cut in the butter until crumbly and scrape the crumb mixture into a bowl. You may process the mixture in a food processor. Whisk the ice water, sour cream and lemon juice in a bowl until blended. Add the sour cream mixture to the crumb mixture and mix with a fork until a dough forms, adding additional ice water as needed for the desired consistency. Let rest at room temperature for 30 minutes. You may flatten the dough, wrap in plastic wrap and store in the refrigerator for 8 to 10 hours for future use.

Preheat the oven to 400 degrees. Roll the dough into a 12-inch (or larger) round on a lightly floured surface. Place the round on a greased baking sheet with sides. You may prepare up to this point and store in the refrigerator until needed.

Combine the mozzarella cheese, fontina cheese and basil in a bowl and mix well. Sprinkle the cheese mixture over the round to within 2 inches of the edge. Arrange the tomato slices slightly overlapping over the cheese and sprinkle with salt and pepper. Fold the uncovered edge of the round over the tomatoes and cheese, pleating to make fit. There will be an open hole in the center.

Bake for 35 to 45 minutes or until golden brown. Let stand for 5 minutes and remove the galette to a serving platter. Cut into wedges and serve hot or at room temperature.

Serves 6

tomato pie

Delightful side dish or a fabulous vegetarian main course.

5   or 6 tomatoes, peeled and
     thickly sliced
1   baked (9-inch) pie shell, cooled
1   (16-ounce) can tomato bits with
     garlic, oregano and basil,
     drained
1/2 cup pine nuts, toasted
1/4 cup pesto
1   garlic clove, minced
2   tablespoons chopped fresh basil
1   teaspoon oregano
11/2 to 2 cups (6 to 8 ounces) mixed
     shredded cheeses (Monterey
     Jack and Cheddar cheese)

Preheat the oven to 350 degrees. Arrange the tomato slices over the bottom of the pie shell. Mix the tomato bits, pine nuts, pesto, garlic, basil and oregano in a bowl and spoon over the tomato slices. Sprinkle with the cheese.

Bake for 25 to 30 minutes or until brown and bubbly. Let stand for 5 minutes before cutting into wedges. Serve immediately.

Serves 8

california corn torta

Corn bread with a twist.

2 cups yellow cornmeal
2 tablespoons sugar
1 tablespoon baking powder
1 tablespoon salt
2 (15-ounce) cans cream-style corn
1 (15-ounce) can whole kernel corn, drained
6 eggs, lightly beaten
1 cup small curd cottage cheese
1/2 cup vegetable oil
1/2 cup sour cream
1 (21-ounce) can green chiles, drained
2 cups (8 ounces) shredded Monterey Jack cheese
2 cups (8 ounces) shredded Cheddar cheese

Preheat the oven to 375 degrees. Combine the cornmeal, sugar, baking powder and salt in a bowl and mix well. Stir in the corn, eggs, cottage cheese, oil and sour cream.

Spread 1/2 of the batter in a buttered 9×13-inch baking pan. Slit the green chiles lengthwise and arrange flat over the batter. Sprinkle with the Monterey Jack cheese and Cheddar cheese and spread with the remaining batter. Bake for 50 to 60 minutes or until puffed, brown and firm.

Serves 8

french toast with orange syrup

This is so good, you'll wish every day was Saturday.

FRENCH TOAST

1	unsliced loaf white bread
10	eggs
1	cup half-and-half
1/8	teaspoon vanilla extract
	Confectioners' sugar

ORANGE SYRUP

1	cup packed brown sugar
1/2	cup orange juice
2	tablespoons grated orange zest

TIP *Serve with a side of berries, and garnish with fresh mint.*

TOAST Cut three 1-inch slices from the bread loaf and trim the crusts. Arrange the slices in a single layer in a 2-inch-deep dish. Whisk the eggs, half-and-half and vanilla in a bowl until blended and pour over the bread, turning to coat. Chill, covered, for 8 to 10 hours.

Bake the bread slices on a lightly greased griddle or in a nonstick skillet for 8 to 10 minutes or until golden brown on both sides. Sprinkle with confectioners' sugar.

SYRUP Combine the brown sugar, orange juice and orange zest in a saucepan and mix well. Simmer over low heat until of a syrup consistency, stirring occasionally. Serve warm with the French toast. Store the leftover syrup in the refrigerator. You may substitute a mixture of 1/4 cup orange juice and 1/4 cup Grand Marnier for the orange juice.

Serves 3

french toast with orange syrup

gingerbread cake

Not just for the holidays. This is divine anytime of the year (or day)!

STREUSEL TOPPING

1	cup packed dark brown sugar
1/4	cup flour
1	to 1 1/2 cups chopped nuts (optional)
1	tablespoon cinnamon
1/4	cup (1/2 stick) butter or margarine, melted

CAKE

2 1/4	cups flour
1	cup dark molasses
3/4	cup hot water
1/2	cup shortening
1/4	cup sugar
1	egg, at room temperature
1	teaspoon baking soda
1	teaspoon ginger
1	teaspoon cinnamon
1/4	teaspoon salt (optional)

TOPPING   Combine the brown sugar, flour, nuts and cinnamon in a bowl and mix well. Add the butter to the brown sugar mixture and stir until crumbly.

CAKE   Preheat the oven to 325 degrees. Combine the flour, molasses, hot water, shortening, sugar, egg, baking soda, ginger, cinnamon and salt in a mixing bowl. Beat at low speed for 30 seconds, scraping the bowl occasionally.

Pour the batter into a greased and floured 9×9-inch baking pan and mound the topping in the middle. Bake for 45 to 50 minutes or until the edges pull from the sides of the pan.

Serves 9

gingerbread cake

golden harvest muffins

So Cali—healthy, fruity, and too, too pretty.

2   cups all-purpose flour
2   cups whole wheat flour
2   cups sugar
4   teaspoons baking soda
4   teaspoons cinnamon
1   teaspoon salt
1/2   teaspoon ground cloves
1 1/2 cups vegetable oil
1/2   cup milk
3   eggs, lightly beaten
4   teaspoons vanilla extract
4   cups shredded peeled apples
1   cup shredded carrots
1   cup shredded coconut
1   cup raisins
1   cup chopped walnuts

Preheat the oven to 350 degrees. Combine the all-purpose flour, whole wheat flour, sugar, baking soda, cinnamon, salt and cloves in a bowl and mix well. Add the oil, milk, eggs and vanilla and stir just until moistened. Fold in the apples, carrots, coconut, raisins and walnuts.

Fill nonstick muffin cups or paper-lined muffin cups 3/4 full. Bake for 20 to 25 minutes or until the muffins test done.

Makes 3 dozen muffins

citrus salad

Perhaps the ultimate taste of California—and it sure beats taking vitamins.

SALAD

1 blood orange, peeled
1 large navel orange, peeled
1 large pink grapefruit, peeled
2 Meyer lemons, peeled
2 tangerines, peeled

CITRUS DRESSING AND
ASSEMBLY

1 tablespoon sherry vinegar
1 tablespoon canola oil or walnut
  oil (optional)
1 tablespoon fructose
1/2 teaspoon freshly ground pepper
2 tablespoons julienned
  fresh basil
4 cups mixed lettuce or mesclun
  Grated zest of 1 orange

SALAD Section the fruit over a bowl, reserving the juices for the dressing. Squeeze any leftover pulp to extract additional juice. Remove the seeds from the fruit.

DRESSING Pour enough of the reserved fruit juices to measure 1/2 cup into a bowl. Whisk in the vinegar, canola oil, fructose and pepper. Stir in the basil. You may add additional fructose to the dressing if the fruit is slightly tart.

ASSEMBLY Divide the greens evenly among 4 chilled salad plates. Arrange the citrus sections on the greens and drizzle with the dressing. Sprinkle with the orange zest.

Serves 4

There's no better
break in the middle
of a busy day than
a fun lunch with
girlfriends.

lunch

We San Diegans have our own take on the traditional power lunch: we don't believe in it. Here's the thing: it's hard to have an attitude when you're sitting on a beautiful patio, surrounded by glowing red-and-purple bougainvillea and flowering birds of paradise, looking at a parade of jewel-bright salads, fruit, and seafood. So, we choose to think of lunch as a time to regroup, recharge, and rethink our day. If we happen to close a deal at the same time...well, who says we women can't do it all?

Of course, in this day and age, there is definitely an eat-at-your-desk component to life. We've got you covered there, too: whether you're typing with one hand and holding a Shrimp Salad Pita in the other or zooming up the 5 with a Chicken and Arugula Sandwich in the passenger seat, life on the run is no reason not to nourish yourself. And on the social side? In our opinion, there's no better break in the middle of a busy day than a fun lunch with girlfriends, comparing notes and strategies and just plain catching up. And, although the cliché of San Diego as being 74 degrees and sunny every day is just that, it is true that it's usually pretty warm by noon, so we like to don our shades and soak up a little Vitamin D while we eat, and we definitely like to keep it casual.

For the San Diego hostess-at-home, it's easy to get creative with fun salads featuring super-fresh, just-picked avocados, tomatoes from the world-renowned Chino Farm, and great, varied local lettuces. Feeling a little bit adventurous? Hit Convoy Street, home to our thriving Asian markets, and fill up your cart with mysterious, deliciously fresh Chinese vegetables and great won ton and rice wrappers to take home for your guests.

Whatever you do, whether you're working, socializing, or wrangling a herd of toddlers (they love our Carrot and Orange Soup, by the way), just don't forget to take a moment in the middle of the day to stop, take a deep breath, and center yourself...there, that wasn't so hard, was it? Now on with the day!

lunch menus

seaside picnic
chicken and arugula sandwiches
green beans with gruyère
california potato salad
the best sugar cookies (Dessert, p. 187)

Forget any outdated notions of soggy sandwiches and bland veggies in dreary Tupperware—this is the New Picnic. These zingy offerings will be a hit with all ages—serve on vivid, primary-color paper plates for added eye appeal.

before the races
salmon burgers
lemon dilly rice salad
ultimate sangria (Tea, p. 96)

This menu never fails to impress even the most languid guest. This lunch is bursting with fresh flavor, is full of spirit, and is light, light, light. A great way to fuel-and-go with both style and substance.

family get-together
fresh corn and tomato salad
fish tacos
lemon bars (Tea, p. 106)

This is casual California dining at its best. Fish tacos, the signature San Diego dish, are fun for kids of all ages to assemble themselves, and are spectacular when paired with our super-fresh salad. Add a zingy citrus note for dessert—perfection!

lunch with the girls
carrot and orange soup
tuna niçoise with aïoli
hot and spicy gingersnaps (Tea, p. 108)

This great make-ahead menu will leave you and your girlfriends satisfied and happy without feeling overly full. More importantly, it lets you get the good stuff down you while you dish the dirt.

carrot and orange soup

Your guests will "drink" their vegetables with delight. Be prepared for rave reviews.

1/4 cup (1/2 stick) unsalted butter
2 1/2 cups chopped yellow onions
12 large carrots, peeled and chopped
5 cups chicken stock
1 cup fresh orange juice with pulp
Salt and pepper to taste
Grated zest of 1/2 orange
1/8 teaspoon cinnamon (optional)

TIP   *To get more juice from a lemon, lime, or orange, microwave on High for thirty seconds.*

Heat the butter in a large saucepan. Cook the onions in the butter over low heat for 25 minutes or until tender, stirring occasionally. Add the carrots and stock to the onion mixture and mix well. Simmer for 30 minutes or until the carrots are tender, stirring occasionally. Reserve 1 cup of the stock.

Remove the solids to a blender or food processor using a slotted spoon. Add a small amount of the hot stock and process until puréed. Return the purée to the saucepan and mix well. Stir in the orange juice and reserved stock. Season with salt and pepper and stir in the orange zest. Simmer just until heated through, stirring occasionally. Ladle into soup bowls and sprinkle with the cinnamon.

Serves 6

pumpkin chile soup

A special fall party surprise with a luxurious spicy-sweet flavor.

1	medium-large onion, chopped
2	garlic cloves, chopped
1	tablespoon butter
4	cups chicken stock
1	(15-ounce) can pumpkin purée
1/4	cup dry sherry
1 1/2	teaspoons red chile flakes, or 1/2 teaspoon hot red chile flakes
1/2	teaspoon black pepper
1/2	teaspoon sugar
1/4	teaspoon allspice
1	cup half-and-half

TIP   *For an easy way to spice up a traditional Thanksgiving dinner, serve this delicious soup as a wonderful first course treat.*

Sauté the onion and garlic in the butter in a saucepan over medium heat until the onion is tender. Combine the stock, pumpkin, sherry, red chile flakes, black pepper, sugar and allspice in a bowl and mix well. Stir the pumpkin mixture into the onion mixture and bring to a boil; reduce the heat.

Simmer, covered, for 30 minutes, stirring occasionally. Remove from the heat and let stand until cool. Process the pumpkin mixture in batches in a blender or food processor until puréed. Return the purée to the saucepan and stir in the half-and-half. Cook just until heated through, stirring occasionally. Ladle into soup bowls.

Serves 4

chicken enchilada soup

SoCal meets Southwest and the result? Olé!

6	tablespoons virgin olive oil or vegetable oil
7	(6-inch) tortillas, cut into halves and cut into $1/4$-inch strips
1	onion, chopped
4	large garlic cloves, crushed
1	tablespoon paprika
2	teaspoons cumin
1	teaspoon coriander
$1/4$	teaspoon cayenne pepper
$1^1/2$	quarts canned reduced-sodium chicken broth
3	cups canned crushed tomatoes in thick purée
2	bay leaves
$2^1/2$	teaspoons salt
$1/4$	cup lightly packed fresh cilantro
$1^3/4$	pounds boneless skinless chicken breasts, chopped
1	avocado, chopped
4	ounces Cheddar cheese, shredded
3	tablespoons chopped fresh cilantro (optional)
4	to 8 lime wedges

TIP   *If you accidentally add too much salt, simply put a cut raw potato into the stockpot while cooking. Keep tasting, and don't forget to throw out the potato once it has done its work.*

Heat the olive oil in a large heavy saucepan over medium-high heat. Add $1/2$ of the tortilla strips. Cook for 1 minute or until golden brown and crisp, stirring frequently. Remove the strips with tongs or a slotted spoon and drain on paper towels. Repeat the process with the remaining tortilla strips, reserving the pan drippings. Reduce the heat to medium-low.

Cook the onion, garlic, paprika, cumin, coriander and cayenne pepper in the reserved pan drippings for 5 minutes, stirring frequently. Stir in the broth, tomatoes, bay leaves, salt, $1/4$ cup cilantro and $1/3$ of the tortilla strips. Bring to a simmer.

Simmer for 30 minutes, stirring occasionally. Discard the bay leaves. Purée the soup in batches in a blender. Return to the saucepan. Stir in the chicken. Bring the soup to a simmer. Simmer for 4 to 5 minutes or until the chicken is cooked through, stirring occasionally. Stir in the avocado.

To serve, divide the remaining tortilla strips evenly among 4 soup bowls and sprinkle with the cheese. Ladle the soup over the top and sprinkle with 3 tablespoons cilantro. Serve with the lime wedges.

Serves 4

white bean chicken chili

When you need something for everyone. Children, men, your girlfriends. . .they'll all come back for more.

1	pound dried large white beans
6	cups chicken broth
2	garlic cloves, minced
2	onions, chopped
1	tablespoon vegetable oil
2	(4-ounce) cans chopped green chiles
2	teaspoons cumin
1 1/2	teaspoons oregano
1/2	teaspoon cayenne pepper
4	cups chopped cooked chicken breasts
3	cups (12 ounces) shredded Monterey Jack cheese

TIP   *To take away the "tin can" taste from canned green chiles, rinse them and dry sauté in a nonstick skillet for a few minutes before adding to the dish.*

Sort and rinse the beans. Combine the beans with enough water to cover generously in a bowl. Let stand for 8 to 10 hours. Drain and rinse. Combine the beans, broth, garlic and 1 of the onions in a stockpot and mix well. Bring to a boil; reduce the heat. Simmer for 3 hours or until the beans are tender, stirring occasionally and adding additional broth if needed for the desired consistency.

Sauté the remaining onion in the oil in a skillet until tender. Stir in the green chiles, cumin, oregano and cayenne pepper. Add the onion mixture to the bean mixture and mix well. Stir in the chicken and simmer for 1 hour longer, stirring occasionally. Ladle into chili bowls and sprinkle with the cheese. Substitute canned beans for the dried beans and reduce the cooking time to 45 to 60 minutes.

Serves 8 to 10

avocado salad

So simple and so good. Guacamole for grown-ups.

1/3	cup finely minced onion
1/4	cup chopped green onions
1/4	cup chopped fresh cilantro
1	small tomato, seeded and chopped
1	cucumber, peeled
1/4	cup fresh lime juice
2	tablespoons olive oil
1/2	teaspoon salt
1/4	teaspoon ground pepper
3	ripe avocados, coarsely chopped
6	romaine leaves

TIP   *If your avocados resemble bullets, you can fast-ripen them by placing in a closed paper bag at room temperature. To speed up the process even more, throw an apple into the bag, and you'll have your own little hothouse.*

Combine the onion, green onions, 1/4 cup cilantro and tomato in a bowl. Cut the cucumber lengthwise into halves and scoop out the seeds with a spoon. Cut crosswise into thin slices and add to the vegetable mixture; toss gently. Add the lime juice, olive oil, salt and pepper and stir until coated. Fold in the avocados.

Arrange 1 romaine leaf on each of 6 salad plates. Top evenly with the avocado mixture. Garnish with sprigs of cilantro. Serve immediately.

Serves 6

goat cheese and tomato salad

We just couldn't leave this one out—very special, virtually foolproof, and truly delicious.

BALSAMIC DIJON VINAIGRETTE

6   tablespoons olive oil
2   tablespoons balsamic vinegar
1   teaspoon mild Dijon mustard
1   garlic clove, finely chopped
1/2   teaspoon salt
    Freshly ground pepper to taste

SALAD

3   Roma tomatoes or small vine-ripened tomatoes, chopped
1   small Haas avocado, chopped
1/2   cup dried cranberries
11/2 to 2 ounces goat cheese, crumbled
1/4   cup pine nuts, toasted
1   head butter lettuce or red or green leaf lettuce, torn into bite-size pieces and chilled
    Freshly ground pepper to taste

VINAIGRETTE   Combine the olive oil, vinegar, mustard, garlic, salt and pepper in a jar with a tight-fitting lid and seal tightly. Shake to mix.

SALAD   Combine the tomatoes, avocado, cranberries, goat cheese, pine nuts and 1/4 cup of the vinaigrette in a bowl and toss gently to coat. Let stand for 10 minutes. Add the lettuce to the tomato mixture and toss to combine. Divide the salad evenly among 4 salad plates and sprinkle with freshly ground pepper. Serve immediately.

Serves 4

fresh corn and tomato salad

A valentine to California—this is what it's all about.

12 large ears of white corn
7 tablespoons olive oil
2 tablespoons finely chopped
 garlic
1 cup packed julienned fresh
 basil
10 Roma tomatoes, chopped
3 tablespoons balsamic vinegar
 Salt and pepper to taste

TIP *As a change to Roma tomatoes, take advantage of the summer season by halving ripe cherry or sweet grape tomatoes to add a super-fresh "pop" to this salad.*

Cut the tops of the corn kernels off the cob with a sharp knife and put into a bowl. Heat 2 tablespoons of the olive oil in each of 2 large skillets. Add $1/2$ of the garlic and $1/2$ of the corn to each of the skillets.

Sauté for 5 minutes or until the corn is tender. Remove from the heat. Add $1/2$ of the basil to each skillet and mix well. Spoon the corn mixture into 2 large bowls. Cool slightly, stirring occasionally. Add $1/2$ of the remaining olive oil, $1/2$ of the tomatoes, $1/2$ of the vinegar and $1/2$ of the remaining basil to each bowl and mix gently. Season with salt and pepper. Chill, covered, for 3 to 8 hours.

Serves 10

fresh corn and tomato salad

black and white bean salad

Fresh and delicious with a healthy kick. Who could ask for anything more?

SUN-DRIED TOMATO DRESSING

3   oil-pack sun-dried tomatoes, finely chopped

2   tomatoes, seeded and finely chopped

1/4   cup chopped fresh cilantro

1   shallot, minced

2   tablespoons white wine vinegar

1/2   cup olive oil

Salt and pepper to taste

SALAD

2   (15-ounce) cans black beans, drained and rinsed

2   (15-ounce) cans white beans, drained and rinsed

1   mango, peeled and chopped

1   cucumber, peeled, seeded and chopped

DRESSING Combine the sun-dried tomatoes, fresh tomatoes, cilantro and shallot in a bowl and mix well. Stir in the vinegar. Add the olive oil gradually, whisking constantly until mixed. Season with salt and pepper.

SALAD Combine the beans, mango and cucumber in a large salad bowl and mix well. Add the dressing and toss to coat. Let stand at room temperature for 30 minutes before serving.

Serves 12

california potato salad

Comfort food at its best, with an elegant artichoke touch.

3   pounds unpeeled small new
    potatoes
    Salt to taste
1   cup mayonnaise
2   tablespoons red wine vinegar
2   tablespoons Dijon mustard
1   tablespoon lemon pepper
1   tablespoon snipped fresh dill
    weed, or 2 to 3 teaspoons
    dried dill weed, crushed
2   (6-ounce) jars marinated
    artichoke hearts, drained and
    sliced
3/4 cup finely chopped onion
4   hard-cooked eggs, chopped
2   tablespoons chopped dill pickle

Combine the potatoes and salt with enough water to cover in a saucepan and cover. Bring to a boil and boil for 20 minutes or until tender; drain. Cool slightly and cut into bite-size pieces.

Combine the mayonnaise, vinegar, mustard, lemon pepper and dill weed in a bowl and mix well. Fold the potatoes, artichokes, onion, eggs and pickle into the mayonnaise mixture. Chill, covered, for 4 to 24 hours. Stir gently before serving.

Serves 16

tomato and bread salad

Just try this once, and we know you'll be hooked for life.

1/2 fresh large loaf Italian semolina
bread (ciabatta), crusts trimmed

5 (about) ripe tomatoes

1/4 cup olive oil

1 bunch scallions, thinly sliced

1 garlic clove, finely chopped

2 tablespoons chopped fresh
Italian parsley

2 teaspoons chopped fresh basil

1 pickled green chile
(pepperoncini), finely chopped

1/2 teaspoon salt

TIP   *Never store tomatoes in the refrigerator. Store stem side down on the kitchen counter, and they will stay fresher longer.*

Preheat the oven to 300 degrees. Cut enough of the bread into 1/2-inch cubes to measure 1 1/2 cups. Spread the bread cubes in a single layer on a baking sheet. Toast for 10 minutes. Let stand until cool.

Seed and chop enough of the tomatoes to measure 2 cups. Combine the tomatoes, olive oil, scallions, garlic, parsley, basil, green chile and salt in a bowl and mix well. Add the bread cubes to the tomato mixture 30 minutes before serving and toss to mix.

Serves 6 to 8

lemon dilly rice salad

Do not let the simple ingredients fool you. This is really, really good.

2   cups water
     Salt to taste
1   cup white long-grain rice
1/2 small red onion, finely chopped
3   tablespoons red wine vinegar
     Juice of 1 lemon
2   tablespoons olive oil
1 1/2 teaspoons minced garlic
1   teaspoon salt
1/4 teaspoon freshly ground pepper
1/4 cup coarsely chopped fresh
     dill weed
     Grated zest of 1 lemon
1   tablespoon coarsely chopped
     fresh dill weed

TIP   *A few drops of lemon juice added to simmering rice will keep the grains separate.*

Bring the water and salt to taste to a boil in a saucepan. Stir in the rice and return to a boil; reduce the heat to low. Cook, uncovered, for 14 to 15 minutes or until the rice is tender; drain. Cover to keep warm.

Combine the onion and vinegar in a bowl and mix well. Let stand for 5 minutes. Drain, reserving the onion and discarding the vinegar. Whisk the lemon juice, olive oil, garlic, 1 teaspoon salt and pepper in a small bowl. Combine the lemon mixture, hot rice, reserved onion, 1/4 cup dill weed and lemon zest in a serving bowl and toss to mix. Sprinkle with 1 tablespoon dill weed and serve immediately.

Serves 4

lemony orzo salad

A great new take on the standard pasta salad and a star at the buffet table.

1	cup orzo
1/3	cup chopped zucchini
1/3	cup chopped red onion
1/3	cup minced fresh parsley
3	tablespoons fresh lemon juice
1	tablespoon minced fresh basil, or 1 teaspoon dried basil
1	tablespoon olive oil
2	teaspoons minced fresh mint
1/2	teaspoon salt
1/4	teaspoon pepper
1	cup chopped tomato
1/3	cup crumbled feta cheese
2	tablespoons chopped kalamata olives

Cook the pasta using the package directions, omitting the salt and butter; drain. Combine the pasta, zucchini and onion in a bowl and toss to mix. Whisk the parsley, lemon juice, basil, olive oil, mint, salt and pepper in a bowl until mixed. Add the pasta mixture to the olive oil mixture and toss to coat. Stir in the tomato, cheese and olives. Serve at room temperature or chilled.

Serves 6

chinese chicken salad

Sweet and sour, crunchy, and yummy. Great for lunch with the girls.

SOY SESAME DRESSING

1/4 cup sugar

1/4 cup soy sauce

3 tablespoons peanut butter

3 tablespoons sesame oil

2 tablespoons vegetable oil

4 teaspoons white vinegar

1/2 teaspoon cayenne pepper

SALAD

3 cups chopped cooked chicken breasts, shredded

1 large head iceberg lettuce, trimmed and torn

3 or 4 green onions with tops, chopped

1/4 cup sesame seeds, toasted

1/4 cup slivered almonds, toasted

1/2 package won ton wrappers, cut into 1/4-inch strips, fried and drained

TIP   *To keep your salad crisp, place an inverted saucer in the bottom of the salad bowl. The excess dressing will drain under the saucer, and you will never have limp greens again.*

DRESSING   Whisk the sugar, soy sauce, peanut butter, sesame oil, vegetable oil, vinegar and cayenne pepper in a bowl until blended.

SALAD   Mix the chicken, lettuce, green onions, sesame seeds, almonds and won tons in a salad bowl. Add the desired amount of dressing and toss to coat. Serve immediately.

Serves 6 to 8

summer salad

California sunshine on a plate. A delicious main-dish salad any time of the year.

DIJON VINAIGRETTE

1/4 cup olive oil
3 tablespoons white wine vinegar
1¹/2 tablespoons Dijon mustard
    Salt and pepper to taste

SALAD

1¹/2 cups chopped grilled
    chicken breasts
2 ripe tomatoes, chopped
1 head green leaf lettuce, torn
1 head red leaf lettuce, torn
1 large avocado, chopped
1/3 cup pine nuts, toasted
1/4 cup (1 ounce) shredded
    mozzarella cheese

TIP *Marinate all of the ingredients
except the lettuce for a delicious, yet
crisp, salad.*

VINAIGRETTE   Combine the olive oil, vinegar, mustard, salt and pepper in a jar with a tight-fitting lid and seal tightly. Shake to mix. Chill until serving time.

SALAD   Toss the chicken, tomatoes, lettuce, avocado, pine nuts and cheese in a salad bowl. Add the vinaigrette and mix until coated. Serve immediately.

Serves 8

To toast whole nuts in the oven, spread the nuts in a single layer on a baking sheet and toast at 350 degrees for fifteen minutes, stirring twice. For sliced or slivered nuts, toast for ten minutes. To toast on the stovetop, heat a heavy cast-iron skillet over high heat for four minutes. Turn off the heat and add one cup of whole, sliced, or slivered nuts to the skillet. Stir constantly for one to three minutes or until the nuts color.

sea scallop salad with citrus vinaigrette

So attractive and tasty, with an unexpected citrus zip.

CITRUS VINAIGRETTE

1/4 cup fresh orange juice
1   small shallot, finely chopped
2   teaspoons freshly grated
     gingerroot, puréed
     Juice of 1 lime
2   tablespoons fresh lemon juice
1/4 to 1/3 cup olive oil
     Salt and freshly ground pepper
     to taste

SALAD

20   sea scallops (about 1 pound)
2   tablespoons olive oil
     Salt and freshly ground pepper
     to taste
4   large handfuls frisée or mixed
     baby salad greens
2   mangoes, peeled and chopped
5   scallions, trimmed and thinly
     sliced diagonally
3/4 cup slivered almonds, toasted

VINAIGRETTE Combine the orange juice, shallot, ginger purée, lime juice and lemon juice in a small bowl and mix well. Let stand for 10 to 15 minutes. Strain the juice mixture into a bowl, discarding the solids. Whisk the olive oil, salt and pepper into the juice mixture until blended.

SALAD Rinse the scallops and pat dry. Remove the "feet" (the small muscle sometimes found on the side of the scallop) and discard. Heat the olive oil in a large sauté pan until almost smoking. Add the scallops to the hot oil and sprinkle with salt and pepper. Cook for 1 minute and turn. Cook for 1 minute longer or until translucent in the center. Remove from the heat.

Toss the frisée, mangoes, scallions and almonds with the desired amount of vinaigrette in a salad bowl. Divide the frisée mixture evenly among 4 plates. Top each serving with 5 scallops and serve immediately with the remaining vinaigrette.

Serves 4

tuna niçoise with aïoli

A modern Southern California take on a timeless French favorite.

BALSAMIC VINAIGRETTE

1	tablespoon Dijon mustard
3	tablespoons balsamic vinegar
1/8	teaspoon salt
1/8	teaspoon pepper
4	to 6 tablespoons olive oil

AÏOLI

2	garlic cloves
1	tablespoon olive oil
3/4	cup mayonnaise

SALAD

1/2	pint cherry tomatoes, halved
	Salt and freshly ground pepper to taste
4	(6-ounce) tuna steaks
1/4	cup olive oil
	Vegetable oil
12	ounces fresh green beans, trimmed
4	generous handfuls mixed salad greens
	Olive oil to taste
1/2	cup pitted black olives, cut into halves (preferably kalamata)

TIP   *Store lettuce in a brown paper bag in the refrigerator, and you will greatly increase its life.*

VINAIGRETTE   Spoon the mustard into a small bowl. Whisk in the vinegar, salt and pepper. Add the olive oil gradually, whisking constantly until blended. Taste, adding additional vinegar or oil if needed for the desired flavor or consistency.

AÏOLI   Combine the garlic and olive oil in a food processor and process until puréed. Add the mayonnaise and process just until blended.

SALAD   Preheat the grill to medium. Season the tomatoes with salt and pepper and toss with 1 tablespoon of the vinaigrette in a bowl. Coat the surface of the tuna with 1/4 cup olive oil and sprinkle with salt and pepper. Let stand at room temperature for 30 minutes.

Coat the hot grill rack with vegetable oil and arrange the tuna on the rack. Grill until a thin band of pink remains on the inside of the tuna, turning 2 or 3 times. Cool to room temperature. You may cook the tuna in a grill pan on the stovetop if desired. Cook the green beans in boiling salted water in a saucepan until tender-crisp; drain. Plunge the beans into a bowl of ice water to stop the cooking process. Drain and pat dry.

To serve, toss the salad greens in a bowl with enough of the vinaigrette to lightly coat the leaves. Divide the greens evenly among plates. Flake the tuna into a bowl and toss with olive oil to taste, salt and pepper. Mound some of the tuna mixture in the center of each plate. Surround the mounded tuna with green beans, cherry tomatoes and olives. Top with a dollop of the aïoli and garnish with a lemon wedge.

Serves 4 to 6

tuna niçoise with aïoli

vinaigrette for all seasons

Trust us! You will never go back to the bottled vinaigrettes again.

2/3 cup virgin olive oil
1/2 cup cream
1 egg, beaten
5 teaspoons white wine vinegar
2 teaspoons minced garlic
2 teaspoons sea salt
1 teaspoon freshly ground
white pepper
1 teaspoon Dijon mustard
1/2 teaspoon dry mustard
1/8 teaspoon sugar (optional)
1 hard-cooked egg, minced
2 tablespoons chopped
black olives
1 tablespoon chopped
fresh chives
1 tablespoon chopped
fresh parsley
1 tablespoon minced drained
capers

Combine the olive oil, cream, egg, vinegar, garlic, salt, white pepper, Dijon mustard, dry mustard and sugar in a jar with a tight-fitting lid and seal tightly. Shake to mix. Add the hard-cooked egg, olives, chives, parsley and capers to the vinaigrette and shake to mix. Alternatively, pour the vinaigrette over blanched summer vegetables and sprinkle with the hard-cooked egg, olives, chives, parsley and capers. Store leftovers in the refrigerator.

If you are concerned about using raw eggs, use eggs pasteurized in their shells, which are sold at some specialty food stores, or use an equivalent amount of pasteurized egg substitute.

Makes about 1 1/2 cups

strawberry vinaigrette

A simple, fruity vinaigrette for favorite summer salads.

8 ounces fresh strawberries
3/4 cup vegetable oil
1/3 cup white vinegar
2 tablespoons honey
1 teaspoon sugar
1/2 teaspoon salt
1/4 teaspoon pepper

Combine the strawberries, oil, vinegar, honey, sugar, salt and pepper in a blender. Process until smooth. Serve with salads or as a dip for fresh fruits.

Makes about 1 1/2 to 2 cups

To blanch fresh vegetables, bring a large saucepan of water to a boil. Add the vegetable of choice to the boiling water in batches small enough that the water never stops boiling (this is very important), and cook until tender-crisp. Immediately plunge the blanched vegetable into ice water to stop the cooking process. Softening tough fibers like green beans and broccoli usually takes several minutes.

green beans with gruyère

So good. Makes a satisfying vegetarian entrée with crusty French bread on the side.

1 1/2 pounds fresh green
beans, trimmed and snapped
1/3 cup olive oil
1/4 cup chopped fresh parsley
2 tablespoons white wine vinegar
1 tablespoon Dijon mustard
Salt and pepper to taste
1 cup sliced fresh mushrooms
4 ounces Gruyère cheese,
shredded

Blanch the green beans in boiling water in a saucepan for 1 minute or until tender-crisp; drain. Plunge the green beans into a bowl of ice water; drain. Combine the olive oil, parsley, vinegar, mustard, salt and pepper in a jar with a tight-fitting lid and seal tightly. Shake to mix. Drizzle the olive oil mixture over the green beans in a bowl and toss to coat. Chill, covered, in the refrigerator. Stir in the mushrooms and cheese just before serving.

Serves 4 to 6

chilled asparagus with feta vinaigrette

Simply elegant and always absolutely delicious. A sure-fire winner.

FETA VINAIGRETTE
2 tablespoons crumbled
feta cheese
2 1/2 tablespoons lemon juice
1 1/2 tablespoons orange juice
1 tablespoon water
2 teaspoons Dijon mustard
1 teaspoon olive oil
2 drops of Tabasco sauce

ASPARAGUS AND ASSEMBLY
1 1/4 pounds fresh asparagus spears
1/2 cup chopped red bell pepper

TIP   *When buying asparagus, pick firm, bright green or pale ivory stalks with tight tips.*

VINAIGRETTE   Whisk the cheese, lemon juice, orange juice, water, mustard, olive oil and Tabasco sauce in a bowl until combined. Store, covered, in the refrigerator.

ASPARAGUS   Snap off the woody ends of the asparagus spears. Arrange the spears spoke fashion stem end out on a microwave-safe 12-inch round platter. Cover with plastic wrap and vent.

Microwave on High for 4 minutes or until tender-crisp, rotating the platter 1/2 turn after 2 minutes. Let stand, covered, for 2 minutes. Chill, covered, in the refrigerator.

ASSEMBLY   Arrange the chilled asparagus evenly on 4 serving plates. Drizzle each serving with 2 tablespoons of the vinaigrette and sprinkle with 2 tablespoons of the bell pepper.

Serves 4

mediterranean couscous with roasted vegetables

The best roasted vegetable dish we have tried.

ROASTED VEGETABLES

1	(1-pound) eggplant, cut lengthwise into 8 wedges
2	zucchini, cut lengthwise into 4 wedges
3	large leeks (white and pale green parts), cut lengthwise into halves and cut crosswise into 2$^1/_2$-inch pieces
1	red bell pepper, cut into $^1/_2$-inch strips
10	unpeeled large garlic cloves
3	tablespoons olive oil
2	tablespoons balsamic vinegar
1	tablespoon chopped fresh rosemary
1	tablespoon chopped fresh thyme Salt and pepper to taste

COUSCOUS AND ASSEMBLY

2$^1/_2$	cups water
1$^1/_2$	teaspoons olive oil
1	teaspoon salt
1	(10-ounce) package couscous
$^1/_4$	cup olive oil
1	cup pitted brine-cured black olives, cut into halves
6	tablespoons fresh lemon juice
3	tablespoons drained capers
3	tablespoons julienned fresh basil Salt and pepper to taste

VEGETABLES   Preheat the oven to 400 degrees. Arrange the eggplant, zucchini, leeks, bell pepper and garlic in a single layer on 2 large baking sheets. Brush with the olive oil and vinegar. Sprinkle with the rosemary, thyme, salt and pepper.

Roast for 45 minutes or until the vegetables are tender, turning occasionally. Cool slightly and cut the vegetables into $^3/_4$-inch pieces. Peel the garlic and coarsely chop.

COUSCOUS   Bring the water, 1$^1/_2$ teaspoons olive oil and 1 teaspoon salt to a boil in a medium saucepan. Stir in the couscous. Remove from the heat and cover. Let stand for 5 minutes or until the water is absorbed; fluff with a fork.

ASSEMBLY   Combine the couscous, roasted garlic, roasted vegetables, $^1/_4$ cup olive oil, olives, lemon juice, capers and basil in a bowl and mix well. Season with salt and pepper. Add a warm grilled chicken breast and turn this colorful side dish into a tasty entrée.

Serves 6

portobello sandwiches

A vegetarian entrée the most ardent carnivores will beg for.

6   portobello mushrooms, stems removed

1   cup plus 2 tablespoons olive oil

1/4   cup balsamic vinegar

2   tablespoons red wine vinegar

3   garlic cloves, minced

2   shallots, minced

Salt and freshly ground pepper to taste

Vegetable oil

6   sourdough hoagie buns or small baguettes, split

1 1/2   cups (6 ounces) crumbled goat cheese

12   oil-pack sun-dried tomatoes, drained and cut in halves

24   fresh basil leaves

Arrange the mushrooms in a single layer in a shallow dish. Whisk the olive oil, balsamic vinegar, wine vinegar, garlic, shallots, salt and pepper in a bowl. Drizzle 1/2 of the olive oil mixture over the mushrooms, turning to coat. Marinate at room temperature for 1 hour, turning once or twice; drain.

Preheat the grill to high and coat the grill rack lightly with vegetable oil. Arrange the mushrooms on the prepared grill rack and weigh down with a large skillet. Grill for 4 minutes or until seared on both sides, turning once.

Drizzle 1 tablespoon of the remaining olive oil mixture over the cut side of each bun. Arrange 1 mushroom on the bottom half of each bun. Layer the top halves evenly with the goat cheese, sun-dried tomatoes and basil and place on the bottom halves to form sandwiches. Secure with wooden picks, cut into halves and wrap with foil. Chill until serving time.

Serves 6

roasted vegetable panini

These are so yummy, you will think you are lunching in the hills of Tuscany.

1	red bell pepper, cut into 8 strips
1	yellow bell pepper, cut into 8 strips
1	zucchini, diagonally sliced
1/2	cup thinly sliced fennel
1	small red onion, cut into 8 slices
1	tablespoon chopped fresh rosemary, or 1 teaspoon dried rosemary
1	tablespoon extra-virgin olive oil
1	tablespoon balsamic vinegar
3/4	teaspoon salt
8	ounces semolina bread, sliced lengthwise into fourths and cut into halves
4	(1-ounce) slices provolone cheese

Preheat the oven to 425 degrees. Spray a large roasting pan with nonstick cooking spray. Combine the bell peppers, zucchini, fennel, onion and rosemary in a bowl and mix well. Whisk the olive oil, vinegar and salt in a bowl and drizzle over the vegetable mixture, tossing to coat. Spread the vegetable mixture in the prepared pan.

Roast for 20 to 25 minutes or until tender and brown, stirring occasionally. Cool slightly. Spoon approximately 3/4 cup of the vegetable mixture on 1 side of 4 slices of the bread and top each with 1 slice of the cheese and the remaining bread slices.

Heat a nonstick skillet sprayed with nonstick cooking spray over medium-high heat. Arrange 2 of the sandwiches in the hot skillet and weigh down with a cast-iron skillet. Cook for 2 minutes or until light brown and crisp. Turn the sandwiches with a spatula and weigh down again with a cast-iron skillet. Cook for 2 minutes longer or until the remaining side is brown. Repeat the process with the remaining sandwiches.

Serves 4

roasted vegetable panini

angel hair pasta with lime and arugula

Fresh and healthy, tart and spicy. The ultimate pasta-at-lunchtime dish.

16   ounces angel hair pasta
     Salt to taste
2   tablespoons extra-virgin olive oil
1   tablespoon grated lime zest
2   garlic cloves, finely chopped
1   mild red chile, seeded and
     finely chopped
2   tablespoons salt-pack capers,
     rinsed and drained
8   thin slices prosciutto or bacon,
     cut diagonally into halves
5   ounces arugula, shredded
3   tablespoons fresh lime juice
5   ounces feta cheese, crumbled
     Freshly ground pepper

TIP   *Never rinse pasta unless it will be baked or served cold in a salad. You need the natural starches to help the sauce cling to the pasta.*

Cook the pasta in boiling salted water in a saucepan using the package directions until al dente; drain. Heat the olive oil in a large skillet over medium heat. Stir in the lime zest, garlic, red chile and capers.

Cook for 1 minute or until fragrant, stirring frequently. Add the prosciutto and mix well. Cook for 2 minutes or until the prosciutto is crisp, stirring frequently. Reserve 2 to 3 tablespoons of the prosciutto mixture. Add the pasta to the remaining prosciutto mixture and toss to coat.

Cook just until heated through, stirring frequently. Remove from the heat. Add the arugula and lime juice to the pasta mixture and toss to mix. Spoon the pasta mixture into individual pasta bowls. Drizzle with the reserved prosciutto mixture and sprinkle with the cheese and pepper. Serve immediately.

Serves 4

shrimp and feta pasta

There's a surprising depth of flavor in such an easy dish. Great make-ahead appeal.

1¹/2 pounds shrimp, cooked, peeled and deveined
4 tomatoes, peeled and chopped
8 ounces feta cheese, crumbled
1 bunch green onions, chopped
2 tablespoons chopped olives
2 teaspoons oregano
10 ounces spinach fettuccini

TIP *Add a lump of butter or a few teaspoons of vegetable oil to the water to prevent the pasta from boiling over.*

Combine the shrimp, tomatoes, cheese, green onions and olives in a bowl and mix gently. Marinate, covered, in the refrigerator for 3 to 4 hours, stirring occasionally.

Cook the pasta using the package directions and drain. Add the pasta to the shrimp mixture and toss to mix. Serve immediately.

Serves 6 to 8

shrimp salad pitas

Move over, Fifties-style "League Sandwiches". . .there's a new sheriff in town.

3	pounds small shrimp
2	teaspoons coarse salt
6	tablespoons drained capers
	Grated zest of 3 lemons
6	to 8 tablespoons homemade or commercially prepared mayonnaise
2	tablespoons chopped fresh dill weed
3/4	teaspoon coarse salt
1/2	teaspoon freshly ground pepper
6	pita rounds
12	leaves Boston lettuce
1	cucumber, peeled and thinly sliced
1	red bell pepper, finely chopped
1/2	bunch green onions, finely chopped
1	rib celery, finely chopped
	Hot sauce to taste

Bring enough water to generously cover the shrimp to a boil in a stockpot. Add the shrimp and 2 teaspoons salt. Cook for 4 to 5 minutes or until the shrimp turn pink. Immediately plunge the shrimp into a bowl of ice water. Let stand until cool; drain. Peel and devein the shrimp and place in a bowl. Add the capers, lemon zest and mayonnaise to the shrimp and mix well. Stir in the dill weed, 3/4 teaspoon salt and pepper. Chill, covered, until serving time.

To serve, cut the pita rounds into halves to form pockets. Line each pocket with 1 lettuce leaf and fill with shrimp salad. Top each with the cucumber, bell pepper, green onions, celery and a splash of hot sauce.

Makes 1 dozen pitas

inside-out fish tacos

A fun way to mix it up with San Diego's signature dish.

1/2 cup dry bread crumbs
1 teaspoon chili powder
1/2 teaspoon salt
1/2 teaspoon pepper
1/4 teaspoon cumin
11/2 pounds firm white fish such as
    halibut, sea bass or
    orange roughy
    Vegetable oil
6 flour tortillas
8 ounces fresh tomatoes, chopped
1 onion, finely chopped
3 to 4 cups salsa
3 cups (12 ounces) shredded
    Monterey Jack cheese
    Shredded cabbage

Mix the bread crumbs, chili powder, salt, pepper and cumin in a shallow dish. Cut the fish into 6 equal portions and coat each portion with the bread crumb mixture. Heat enough oil in a skillet to measure 1/2 inch. Fry the fish in the hot oil for 5 minutes per side or until golden brown; drain.

Preheat the oven to 350 degrees. Arrange 3 of the tortillas in a single layer in a 9×13-inch baking dish sprayed with nonstick cooking spray. Top each tortilla with 2 of the fish portions. Layer 1/2 of the tomatoes, 1/2 of the onion and 1/2 of the salsa over the prepared layers and sprinkle with 1 cup of the cheese. Top with the remaining 3 tortillas, remaining tomatoes, remaining onion, remaining salsa and remaining cheese. Bake for 20 minutes or until bubbly and heated through.

Line 6 serving plates with shredded cabbage. Cut the tortilla stacks into halves and arrange 1 half on each plate. Garnish with lime wedges and serve with ranch salad dressing or sour cream. You may also serve with additional salsa, sliced avocados or guacamole and additional warm flour tortillas.

Serves 6

Since 1983, when local boy Ralph Rubio opened up a small stand in Mission Bay, the fish taco has been beloved by San Diegans. We share its history with our neighbor to the south, Ensenada, where residents are fierce about their food. No trip to San Diego would be complete without sampling one of these specialties.

fish tacos

A San Diego staple. We know you will love them too.

BEER BATTER

1	cup flour
1/2	teaspoon garlic powder
1/4	teaspoon red pepper
1/4	teaspoon freshly ground black pepper
1	cup beer

WHITE SAUCE

1/2	cup mayonnaise
1/2	cup plain yogurt

TACOS AND ASSEMBLY

	Vegetable oil for deep-frying
12	(1 1/2-ounce) cod fillets or any white fish fillets
	Salt to taste
1	dozen fresh corn tortillas
	Shredded Cheddar cheese to taste
	Salsa to taste
1	head green cabbage, shredded
	Lime juice to taste

BATTER   Combine the flour, garlic powder, red pepper and black pepper in a bowl and mix well. Whisk the flour mixture into the beer in a bowl until blended.

SAUCE   Mix the mayonnaise and yogurt in a bowl.

TACOS   Heat enough oil in a skillet to 375 degrees to deep-fry the fillets. Rinse the fillets and dip in a bowl of lightly salted cold water. Drain and pat dry with paper towels. Coat the fillets with the batter and fry in batches in the hot oil until crisp and golden brown; do not allow the fillets to touch. Drain on paper towels. Heat the tortillas in a skillet until pliable and warm.

ASSEMBLY   Layer each tortilla with 1 fish fillet, shredded cheese, White Sauce, salsa and cabbage and drizzle with lime juice. Fold over to enclose the filling and serve immediately.

Makes 1 dozen tacos

fish tacos

salmon burgers

Absolutely everyone loves these burgers. They taste as good as they look.

1/2 red onion, finely chopped

1/4 cup olive oil

1 cup dry white wine

1/2 cup fresh lemon juice

1 (4-ounce) jar capers, drained and chopped

2 pounds skinless salmon fillets, bones removed and cut into 1-inch chunks

3 cups fresh ciabatta bread crumbs

2 eggs, lightly beaten

3 tablespoons chopped fresh dill weed

1 1/2 teaspoons salt

3/4 teaspoon pepper

1 tablespoon olive oil

10 hamburger buns, toasted

TIP *For a knockout display at the lunch table, serve these burgers open-faced and topped with slices of heirloom tomatoes in various colors.*

Sauté the onion in 1/4 cup olive oil in a skillet over medium heat for 4 minutes or until tender. Increase the heat to medium-high and stir in the wine, lemon juice and capers. Cook for 12 minutes or until most of the liquid evaporates, stirring frequently. Spoon the onion mixture into a bowl and chill, covered, for 1 hour.

Place the salmon in a food processor and pulse until coarsely ground. Add the ground salmon to the onion mixture and mix well. Stir in the bread crumbs, eggs, dill weed, salt and pepper. Shape the salmon mixture into 10 patties. You may prepare the patties up to 6 hours in advance and store, covered, in the refrigerator.

Heat 1 tablespoon olive oil in a large heavy skillet over medium-high heat. Brown the patties in batches in the olive oil for 2 minutes per side or until cooked through and brown, adding additional olive oil as needed. Serve the salmon burgers on the buns with mayonnaise, lettuce and sliced tomatoes.

Makes 10 burgers

salmon burgers

salmon cakes

Dress 'em up, dress 'em down, these are just good, good, good.

1/2	yellow or red bell pepper, chopped
1	tablespoon olive oil
1/3	cup cream
2	teaspoons chopped fresh chives
2	teaspoons chopped fresh dill weed
2	teaspoons chopped fresh parsley
1/2	teaspoon salt
1/8	teaspoon cayenne pepper
1	egg, lightly beaten
3/4	cup fresh bread crumbs
1/2	cup ground almonds
1	pound salmon tail or end, chopped
	Olive oil

Sauté the bell pepper in 1 tablespoon olive oil in a skillet until tender. You may sauté in water if desired. Combine the sautéed bell pepper, cream, chives, dill weed, parsley, salt and cayenne pepper in a bowl and mix well. Stir in the egg, 1/2 of the bread crumbs and 1/2 of the almonds and fold in the salmon. Shape the salmon mixture into 12 round cakes.

Mix the remaining bread crumbs and remaining almonds in a shallow dish and coat the cakes with the crumb mixture. Chill, covered, for 2 to 3 hours. Sauté the cakes in additional olive oil in a skillet for 2 minutes per side or until golden brown; drain. Serve over mixed salad greens with your favorite seafood sauce.

Makes 1 dozen salmon cakes

pan-fried crab cakes

Worth the work and more. Serve miniature-size crab cakes for pop-in-the-mouth heaven.

1	small onion, finely chopped
2	ribs celery, finely chopped
2	tablespoons unsalted butter
1 1/2	teaspoons dry mustard
1/8	teaspoon cayenne pepper
1	pound lump crab meat, drained and shells removed
1	egg, lightly beaten
2/3	cup fresh bread crumbs
1/4	cup mayonnaise
2	tablespoons chopped fresh mint
2	tablespoons chopped fresh cilantro
1 1/2	teaspoons Old Bay seasoning
1	teaspoon grated lemon zest
	Salt to taste
	Canola oil for frying
	Lemon wedges

TIP   *Don't be cheap about these. It really is important to use fresh crab meat if available, and do not even think about substituting imitation crab sticks.*

Sauté the onion and celery in the butter in a skillet over medium heat for 4 to 5 minutes or until tender but not brown. Stir in the dry mustard and cayenne pepper. Let stand until cool.

Combine the onion mixture, crab meat, egg, bread crumbs, mayonnaise, mint, cilantro, Old Bay seasoning, lemon zest and salt in a bowl and mix gently. Shape the crab meat mixture by 1/3 cupfuls into firm patties. Sauté the patties in canola oil in a skillet for 3 minutes per side or until brown and crisp; drain. Serve warm with lemon wedges. These are great served with the Rémoulade Sauce on page 158.

Makes 8 crab cakes

chicken and arugula sandwiches

Colorful, delicious, and oh-so-simple to make. The best at a beach barbecue.

3   tablespoons plain nonfat yogurt
    or low-fat mayonnaise
4   teaspoons Dijon mustard
1/2 cup chopped arugula
    Freshly ground pepper to taste
2   large red bell peppers
4   (4-ounce) boneless skinless
    chicken breasts
    Salt to taste
1   teaspoon olive oil
6   (5- to 6-inch) baguettes French
    bread or rolls, cut lengthwise
    into halves
2   large bunches arugula

TIP   *Replace the chicken with grilled eggplant slices for a tasty vegetarian option.*

Combine the yogurt and mustard in a bowl and mix well. Stir in 1/2 cup arugula and season with pepper. Store, covered, in the refrigerator for up to 1 day.

Char the bell peppers over a gas flame or broil until the skin is blistered and blackened on all sides. Immediately place the bell peppers in a resealable plastic bag and seal tightly. Allow to steam in the bag for 10 minutes. Peel and seed the bell peppers and cut into 1/2-inch strips.

Sprinkle the chicken with salt and pepper. Brush a nonstick skillet with the olive oil and sauté the chicken in the oil for 4 minutes per side or until cooked through. Cool slightly and slice diagonally into strips.

Spread 2 teaspoons of the yogurt mixture on the cut sides of each bread half. Layer 1 bunch of the arugula and the chicken over the bottom halves. Top with the roasted bell pepper strips, remaining arugula and remaining bread halves. Wrap tightly in plastic wrap and chill for up to 4 hours. To save time, substitute commercially prepared roasted bell peppers for the fresh bell peppers.

Makes 6 sandwiches

chicken and arugula sandwiches

grilled chicken with nectarine guacamole

Nectarines make an unexpectedly delicious addition to a classic flavor pairing.

NECTARINE GUACAMOLE

2   medium to large nectarines, peeled and chopped

1   avocado, chopped into 1/2-inch pieces

2   or 3 green onions, finely chopped

1/4   cup finely chopped fresh cilantro

3   tablespoons fresh lime or orange juice

1   or 2 fresh jalapeño chiles, seeded and finely chopped

1   large garlic clove, finely chopped

1/4   teaspoon salt

CHICKEN

4   boneless skinless chicken breasts

GUACAMOLE   Combine the nectarines, avocado, green onions, cilantro, lime juice, jalapeño chiles, garlic and salt in a bowl and mix well. Chill, covered, in the refrigerator for 1 hour.

CHICKEN   Preheat the grill. Grill the chicken over hot coals until cooked through, turning occasionally. Top each chicken breast with some of the guacamole. You may substitute four 4-ounce red snapper or swordfish fillets for the chicken.

Serves 4

chicken salad sandwiches

Make these workday beauties into lunch-party stars by serving on flaky, fresh, warm croissants.

2 cups chopped cooked chicken
8 ounces seedless grapes, cut into halves
1/2 cup chopped celery
1/2 cup slivered almonds or chopped cashews
1/4 cup water chestnuts, sliced
3/4 cup mayonnaise
1 1/2 to 2 teaspoons curry powder
2 teaspoons soy sauce
2 teaspoons lemon juice
4 (5- to 6-inch) baguettes, French bread or rolls, cut lengthwise into halves

Combine the chicken, grapes, celery, almonds and water chestnuts in a bowl and mix well. Mix the mayonnaise, curry powder, soy sauce and lemon juice in a bowl and stir into the chicken mixture. Chill, covered, for 2 hours or longer. Serve the chicken salad on the bread.

If leftover chicken is not an option for this recipe, marinate 2 chicken breasts in the refrigerator in a mixture of olive oil, lemon juice, garlic, salt and pepper for 1 hour or longer. Bake at 400 degrees for 30 minutes. Cool slightly, chop and add to the salad.

Serves 4

In the summer, we
like to head outside,
ice-down the tea,
spread out the
goodies, and let the
sunshine work
its magic.

tea

While we know how lucky we are to live in one of the world's best climates, the fact is that whether the weather is perfect or not, an early afternoon get-together is something special. Don't let traditional (and, dare we say it, old-fashioned) notions of "afternoon tea" slow you down—we do things a little bit differently these days. (And one of the best things about hosting a tea party is that everything is prepared in advance, leaving you plenty of time to enjoy your guests—and your food!)

In the summer, we like to head outside, ice-down the tea, spread out the goodies, and let the sunshine work its magic. There is nothing like our "Simply Savory" menu set out on a picnic table in the middle of your yard. Just dust off the lawn chairs, and don't fret about anything fussy—there's no need for cut flowers or fancy place settings. Instead, have one of your favorite potted plants as a fun centerpiece, and use terracotta pots or baskets to hold flatware and napkins.

Keeping it casual is our signature here in San Diego, but we also know how to turn it up a notch, if the mood strikes us. For a ladies-only occasion, we love the simplicity and beauty of a more traditional tea, like our "Feeling Fruity" menu. Add a little Champagne to the mix, and you'll be in for more gossip than you can handle!

In the winter, believe it or not, we think that cold afternoons are a treat, and we beg for a good reason to make a fire, wear socks, and curl up with a cup of hot tea. "Going Nutty" is a perfect way to pass a rainy afternoon— why not make it a fun occasion and call up your mom or the sweet neighbor you've been meaning to get to know? Oh, and inviting the cat to sit on your lap is optional.

tea menus

simply savory
herby garlic cheese bread
gouda-stuffed mushrooms
goat cheese tarts
chicken curry finger sandwiches

Tea Recommendations: Savory foods do well with smoky,
assertive black teas and some Asian green teas. Why not try
a cup of black Darjeeling, Assam, or even Lapsang Souchong?

feeling fruity
orange miniature muffins
quick strawberry jam
almond orange wafers
lemon bars

Tea Recommendations: Less hearty black teas and herbal teas go well with fruity food flavors.
Try Earl Grey, Chamomile, Ginseng, or an Oolong tea for best results.

going nutty
biscotti di prato
almond butter cake
hot and spicy gingersnaps

Tea Recommendations: With nutty and spicy foods, you should choose teas to offset the richness
of the food's flavor. Strong, but not sweet, citrus teas are a good choice—try a ginger-peach, cardamon,
or even black tea with a hint of mint.

ultimate sangria

This is the best version we have found for this classic drink.

3	liters red wine (cabernet sauvignon)
2	cups sugar
6	to 8 ounces plain brandy
2	large lemons, thinly sliced
2	large oranges, thinly sliced
2	large apples, sliced
1	to 2 liters citrus-flavor bubbly water (orange or lemon preferred)

Mix the wine, sugar, brandy, lemons, oranges and apples in a large container. Chill, covered, for 18 to 24 hours, stirring occasionally. Just before serving, stir again and taste, adding additional sugar or brandy if desired. It should have a fairly strong flavor and be fairly sweet, almost syrupy. Add 1 liter of the bubbly water, stirring until the sangria has a thinner, more wine-like consistency and adding additional bubbly water as needed. Pour into glasses.

Makes about 4^1/2 quarts

TIP *Eliminate the sugar by choosing a sweet red wine, and add real eye appeal by floating more exotic fruits in the pitcher, like raspberries, nectarine, peach, and pear slices, plum halves, and blackberries. Be creative!*

members' punch

We serve this fun punch at new member and provisional meet and greets.

3	cups sugar
2	cups lemon juice
4	cups drained canned pineapple chunks
1^1/2 quarts ice water	
1	quart Rhine wine or any type inexpensive white wine
1	quart strawberries, lightly sugared
2	large bottles Champagne, chilled

Mix the sugar and lemon juice in a large container and stir until the sugar dissolves. Add the pineapple, ice water and wine and mix well. Chill, covered, until ready to serve. Combine with the strawberries and Champagne in a punch bowl and mix gently. Ladle into punch cups.

Makes 6 quarts

ultimate sangria

La Jolla deserves its reputation as San Diego's jewel-by-the-sea. This village-within-the-city has everything, from tip-top shops to a thriving local café scene. Visitors shouldn't miss the Children's Pool (where seals like to sunbathe), Scripps Pier, the Birch Aquarium, and La Jolla's main shopping drag, Girard Avenue. Don't blame us if you never want to leave.

la jolla lemonade

Pretty in pink. Add vodka if you dare.

1	cup fresh or thawed frozen raspberries
12	cups water
3	cups fresh lemon juice (12 to 15 lemons)
1¹/2	cups sugar
2	teaspoons finely chopped fresh mint

Mash the raspberries lightly with a fork in a large glass or ceramic bowl. Add the water, lemon juice, sugar and mint to the raspberries and mix gently until the sugar dissolves.

Strain the raspberry mixture into a large pitcher, discarding the solids. Chill, covered, in the refrigerator. Pour the lemonade over ice in glasses and garnish with additional raspberries, lemon slices and/or fresh mint leaves.

Serves 14 to 16

spiked watermelon lemonade

Makes a fun adults-only punch.

4	cups puréed seeded watermelon
2	cups water
2	cups fresh lemon juice
1	to 2 cups vodka
1	cup sugar

Combine the watermelon purée, water, lemon juice, vodka and sugar in a pitcher and mix well. Chill, covered, in the refrigerator until serving time. Pour the lemonade over ice in glasses and garnish with lemon slices and sprigs of fresh mint.

Serves 8

gouda-stuffed mushrooms

The only thing that's stuffy at our meetings.

6	ounces pancetta or Canadian bacon, finely chopped
2	tablespoons butter
1	small onion, finely chopped
3	garlic cloves, minced
1	cup packed trimmed fresh spinach, chopped
2	cups (8 ounces) shredded Gouda cheese
3/4	cup fresh bread crumbs
2	tablespoons chopped fresh basil Salt and freshly ground pepper to taste
24	(2-inch) cremini mushroom caps

Preheat the oven to 400 degrees. Sauté the pancetta in a medium skillet over medium heat for 3 minutes or until crisp. Remove the pancetta to a bowl using a slotted spoon. Drain the skillet.

Melt the butter in the same skillet over medium heat. Sauté the onion and garlic in the butter for 3 minutes. Stir in the spinach. Cook just until wilted, stirring occasionally. Return the pancetta to the skillet and mix well. Cool slightly. Stir in the cheese, bread crumbs and basil and season with salt and pepper.

Arrange the mushroom caps in a single layer on a baking sheet. Mound 2 1/2 tablespoons of the cheese mixture in the center of each cap. Bake for 8 minutes. Serve immediately.

Serves 8

To preserve fresh herbs, pick unbruised leaves from their stems and splash with cold water. Pack several tablespoons of the herbs into small paper cups. Fill the cups with enough cold water to cover the herbs and freeze. To use, thaw under running water and proceed as with fresh herbs.

herby garlic cheese bread

So easy. All the taste of Italy with none of the effort.

1/2 cup (1 stick) unsalted butter, softened

1/4 cup (1 ounce) freshly grated Parmesan cheese

3 garlic cloves, minced

1 tablespoon minced fresh basil

1/2 teaspoon minced fresh thyme

1/2 teaspoon minced fresh oregano, or 1/16 teaspoon dried oregano
Salt and freshly ground pepper to taste

1 large loaf French or sourdough French bread, cut lengthwise into halves

1/4 cup (1 ounce) freshly grated Parmesan cheese

Preheat the oven to 400 degrees. Combine the butter, 1/4 cup cheese, garlic, basil, thyme, oregano, salt and pepper in a bowl and mix well. Spread the butter mixture on the cut sides of the bread halves and sprinkle with 1/4 cup cheese.

Cut the bread halves into 2-inch-thick slices approximately 3/4 of the way through but not to the bottom. Wrap each half separately in foil. You may prepare to this point up to 4 hours in advance and store in the refrigerator. Let stand at room temperature for 30 minutes before baking. Arrange the wrapped bread halves on a baking sheet. Bake for 10 to 15 minutes or until bubbly.

Serves 8

goat cheese tarts

So quick and easy. . .and so decadent. Bet you can't eat just one.

1   (12-ounce) package puff pastry, thawed
2   (4-ounce) logs goat cheese
1   egg, beaten
6   sprigs of fresh basil

Preheat the oven to 450 degrees. Cut the pastry into 6 equal portions. Roll each portion into a 6x6-inch square. Cut each cheese log into 3 equal portions.

Arrange each cheese portion on a pastry square. Brush the edges of the pastry with the egg. Draw the sides of the pastry up to form a pyramid. Press the pastry edges together halfway up the sides, leaving the center open. Top each with a sprig of basil.

Arrange the tarts on a baking sheet. Bake for 15 minutes or until the cheese softens and the pastry is golden brown and puffed. Serve warm.

Makes 6 tarts

chicken curry finger sandwiches

A great make-ahead item. Keep double servings ready.

2 cups finely chopped cooked chicken breast
1/2 cup slivered almonds, toasted
1/4 cup chopped celery
1/4 cup chopped water chestnuts
3/4 cup mayonnaise
1/2 teaspoon lemon juice
1/2 teaspoon curry powder
1/2 teaspoon mango chutney

TIP *Add versatility to this dish by serving it as a salad for a fun buffet selection. Chop the chicken, throw in halved grapes and some raisins, and serve over mixed greens—delicious!*

Combine the chicken, almonds, celery and water chestnuts in a bowl and mix well. Stir in the mayonnaise, lemon juice, curry powder and chutney. Chill, covered, in the refrigerator.

Serve open-faced on your favorite bread. For variety, cut bread into interesting shapes using cookie cutters. Garnish with fresh chives and fresh parsley.

Makes about 3 to 4 cups

almond butter cake

The only problem with this cake is how hard it is to stop eating.

1 cup sugar
1/2 cup (1 stick) butter
1 egg
1/2 cup almond paste
1 cup flour
Sliced almonds to taste

TIP *This is a great rich cookie-cake that's a hit served with fresh strawberries in season and whipped cream.*

Preheat the oven to 325 degrees. Beat the sugar and butter in a mixing bowl until creamy. Add the egg and beat until smooth. Mix in the almond paste until blended and stir in the flour.

Spread the batter in a buttered 9-inch round baking dish and sprinkle with almonds. Bake for 35 minutes or until the cake tests done. Cool in the pan for 10 minutes. Remove to a wire rack to cool completely. Slice and garnish as desired.

Serves 8 to 12

To dry lemon or orange zest, grate a lemon or orange or peel into thin strips. Spread the zest on a paper towel or paper plate. Microwave on High for two to three minutes or until dried but not dark, rotating the towel or plate after two minutes. Cool and store in a freezer container in the freezer. Makes about one tablespoon dried zest, which is double the flavor strength of a fresh amount when cooking.

orange miniature muffins

Stack 'em high because they'll disappear in a second.

1 cup sugar
  Juice of 1 orange
  (about 1/2 cup)
2 cups flour, sifted
1 teaspoon baking soda
1 teaspoon salt
1/2 cup (1 stick) butter
1 cup sugar
3/4 cup sour cream
1/2 cup raisins
1/2 cup chopped nuts
1 teaspoon grated orange zest

Preheat the oven to 375 degrees. Combine 1 cup sugar and the orange juice in a bowl and stir until the sugar dissolves. Mix the flour, baking soda and salt together. Beat the butter and 1 cup sugar in a mixing bowl until creamy. Add the sour cream and flour mixture alternately, beating just until moistened after each addition. Fold in the raisins, nuts and orange zest. The batter will be stiff.

Spoon the batter into greased miniature muffin cups. Bake for 12 to 15 minutes or until the muffins test done. Dip the warm muffins in the orange juice mixture and place on a wire rack. Let stand until cool.

Makes 3 dozen miniature muffins

orange miniature muffins

lemon bars

Move over, brownies!

CRUST
1/2 cup (1 stick) butter, softened
1/4 cup confectioners' sugar
1 cup flour

LEMON FILLING
2 eggs
1 cup sugar
2 tablespoons flour
2 tablespoons fresh lemon juice
  Grated zest of 1/2 lemon
  Confectioners' sugar to taste

CRUST   Preheat the oven to 325 degrees. Beat the butter and confectioners' sugar in a mixing bowl until creamy. Add the flour and beat until blended. Pat the flour mixture over the bottom of an 8×8-inch baking pan. Bake for 15 to 20 minutes or until light brown. Maintain the oven temperature.

FILLING   Whisk the eggs in a bowl just until blended. Add the sugar, flour, lemon juice and lemon zest and whisk until mixed. Pour the lemon mixture over the hot baked layer. Bake for 15 to 20 minutes or just until almost set. Sprinkle with confectioners' sugar. Let stand until cool and cut into bars.

Makes 1 dozen bars

To make chocolate biscotti, add four ounces melted sweet dark chocolate to the egg and sugar mixture, then continue as instructed. Almonds with their skins on are good with plain biscotti, but almonds without their skins are best for the chocolate version. Toast almonds in a 350-degree oven for approximately five minutes.

biscotti di prato

Not just for dipping in coffee.

3 eggs, at room temperature
2 egg yolks, at room temperature
2 cups sugar
1 teaspoon vanilla extract
3 3/4 cups flour
1 teaspoon baking powder
2 cups almonds, toasted and coarsely chopped
1/4 to 1/2 cup flour
1 egg, beaten

Preheat the oven to 350 degrees. Combine 3 eggs and the egg yolks in a mixing bowl and beat just until blended. Add the sugar to the eggs gradually, beating constantly until fluffy. Beat in the vanilla until blended. Mix 3 3/4 cups flour and the baking powder together. Add the flour mixture to the egg mixture gradually, beating constantly until blended. Fold in the almonds and 1/4 cup of the flour. Sprinkle the remaining flour on a hard work surface and on your hands.

Divide the dough into 5 equal portions and roll each portion into a log on the floured work surface. Arrange the logs on a buttered and floured cookie sheet and flatten slightly. Brush the logs with 1 beaten egg.

Bake for 30 to 35 minutes. Remove from the oven and place the logs on a cutting board. Cut each log diagonally into 3/4- to 1-inch slices. Arrange the slices in a single layer on the cookie sheet. Return the cookie sheet to the oven. Turn off the oven and let stand with the door closed for 15 minutes. Remove to a wire rack to cool completely. Store in an airtight container.

Makes 3 dozen biscotti

hot and spicy gingersnaps

Heat up any party with these saucy little treats.

$2^1/2$ cups flour

$1^1/2$ teaspoons baking soda

1 teaspoon (or more) ginger

3/4 teaspoon cinnamon

1/2 teaspoon ground cloves

1/2 teaspoon salt

1/2 teaspoon cayenne pepper

1/2 cup (1 stick) unsalted butter, cut into pieces

1 cup packed light brown sugar

1/2 cup sugar

1/3 cup molasses

1/4 cup egg whites (about 2 eggs)

2 to 4 tablespoons sugar

TIP   *Old cut-crystal glasses with patterns on the bottoms make pretty designs on these cookies. Dampen the bottom of one of these glasses with water and dip in sugar. Press gently into the dough for Old World appeal.*

Preheat the oven to 350 degrees. Mix the flour, baking soda, ginger, cinnamon, cloves, salt and cayenne pepper together. Beat the butter in a mixing bowl until light and fluffy. Add the brown sugar and 1/2 cup sugar and beat until blended. Blend in the molasses. Add the egg whites 1/2 at a time, mixing well after each addition. Add the flour mixture 1/3 at a time and beat until blended after each addition.

Spread 2 to 4 tablespoons sugar on a small plate. Shape the dough into 3/4-inch balls and roll in the sugar until lightly coated. Arrange the balls 1 inch apart on a cookie sheet lined with baking parchment. Bake for 8 to 10 minutes or until brown. Cool on the cookie sheet for 2 minutes. Remove to a wire rack to cool completely. Store in an airtight container.

Makes about 4 dozen cookies

almond orange wafers

Delicate and sweet. A taste of sunny climes in a cookie.

1/2   cup (1 stick) butter, softened
1/2   cup sugar
1   egg
1/2   teaspoon almond extract
1/2   teaspoon grated orange zest
3/4   cup flour
1/2   cup sliced almonds

Preheat the oven to 375 degrees. Beat the butter and sugar in a mixing bowl until light and fluffy. Add the egg, flavoring and orange zest and beat until combined. Stir in the flour and almonds.

Drop by teaspoonfuls 3 inches apart onto a greased cookie sheet. Bake for 7 minutes. Cool on the cookie sheet for 2 minutes. Remove to a wire rack to cool completely. Store in an airtight container.

Makes 4 dozen wafers

quick strawberry jam

You will never buy the stuff in a jar again.

1 1/2 pounds fresh strawberries
1   vanilla bean
1/16   teaspoon salt
1/2   cup sugar

Cut the strawberries into quarters and place in a medium saucepan. Split the vanilla bean lengthwise into halves and scrape out the seeds. Add the seeds to the strawberries and mix well. Stir in the salt.

Cook over medium heat for 20 minutes or until the mixture is reduced by half, stirring occasionally. Stir in the sugar. Cook for 15 to 20 minutes longer or until the mixture is reduced to 2 cups, stirring occasionally. Continue cooking if a thicker consistency is desired. The jam will thicken slightly as it cools.

Spoon the jam into a sterilized jar or bowl. Let stand until cool. Store, covered, in the refrigerator for up to 1 month.

Makes 2 cups

Happy hour is the perfect opportunity to savor time spent with friends at the end of the day. Cheers!

happy hour

Maybe it's a California thing—people here go to work early, work hard, and leave early too—but we've never had a very difficult time convincing people to get together for happy hour. There's something appealing about a time of day whose purpose is solely to get us out of the work grind and into the party mood that has universal appeal, especially to us relaxed San Diegans. And for visitors to our wonderful city: whether you're coming home from a full day at our world-famous zoo or drying out from an encounter with Sea World, now is definitely the time to adopt what we like to call the Fiesta Spirit.

But before we get going, we'd like to share one special local tradition that really sets the scene for us and is the signal for happy hour to go, go, go. Every evening around sunset, residents and visitors alike congregate at small viewpoint parks and on boardwalks to watch the sun sink like a fiery stone into the deep blue Pacific. Sweater-wrapped neighbors (we're thin-blooded out here) come out with dogs and drinks to watch Mother Nature's free show before making dinner, while cars pull over to the side of the road at Cardiff State Beach and Carlsbad to take just a minute out of life and search for the elusive "green flash" as night falls.

And then? Well, we usually find that it's time to fire up the blender for a batch of Old Town Margaritas and to throw some coals on the barbecue pit for Teriyaki Strips. Whether you're a Pointer, as we like to call the residents of Point Loma, watching the skyline slowly light up over downtown as you enjoy Spicy Shrimp Cocktail and a side of Guacamole; or a Banker's Hill local watching the night fall over our beautiful Balboa Park, happy hour is the perfect opportunity to savor time spent with friends at the end of the day. Cheers!

Coronado's charm is not exactly a well-kept secret, but we would be remiss if we did not talk about the Hotel del Coronado, an area landmark (and famous Hollywood player in its capacity as the location for *Some Like It Hot* and other films). Here's a tip from the locals. If you rise early, you can view the Navy Seals running on the beach at dawn, which is not only a patriotic sight for sore eyes, but also a great motivator.

coronado cocktail

This fresh, tangy, minty drink packs a real punch.

MINT SYRUP
2 cups water
2 cups sugar
2 quarts fresh mint leaves (about 3 bunches)

COCKTAIL
2 cups fresh lime juice
24 ounces vodka
24 ounces club soda (optional)

TIP *The mint syrup will keep in the freezer for up to three months and is great for impromptu parties.*

SYRUP   Combine the water, sugar and mint leaves in a 3- or 4-quart saucepan. Bring to a simmer over medium-low heat, stirring occasionally. Remove from the heat. Let stand for 30 minutes or until cool. Strain into a pitcher, discarding the solids. Chill for 45 minutes or until cold. You may store the syrup in the refrigerator for up to 7 days.

COCKTAIL   Fill one 8-ounce glass halfway with ice cubes. Add 2 tablespoons of the lime juice and 1 tablespoon of the syrup and stir gently. Add 1 to 2 ounces of the vodka, depending on the preferred alcohol content, and mix well. Garnish with fresh mint. Repeat the process for each serving. For a spritzer effect, add 1 to 2 ounces of the club soda to each cocktail.

Serves 12

socal mojitos

The Cosmopolitan of San Diego. Drink wearing Manolos on the beach.

1 tablespoon sugar
1 ounce boiling water
1 1/2 ounces apple vodka
3/4 ounce fresh lime juice
Club soda

Dissolve the sugar in the boiling water in a small heatproof bowl. Let stand until cool. Combine the cooled syrup, vodka and lime juice in a highball glass filled with ice. Pour in the desired amount of club soda. Garnish with a mint sprig, apple slice and ginger slice.

Serves 1

point loma sangria

An unexpected and refreshing change from wine.

1	(750-milliliter) bottle white wine of choice
2 1/2	cups apple juice
1	cup Triple Sec
2	tablespoons sugar
1	orange, thinly sliced
1/2	lemon, thinly sliced
1	lime, thinly sliced
1	cup raspberries

Combine the wine, apple juice, liqueur, sugar, orange slices, lemon slices, lime slices and raspberries in a large pitcher and press the fruit against the side and bottom of the pitcher to release the juices. Chill, covered, until serving time. The flavor of the sangria is enhanced the longer the wine mixture is allowed to chill. Add ice just before serving. For large parties or groups, double the fruit and use in an ice ring to float in a punch bowl.

Serves 4

lemon drop martini

Tastes like liquid candy and knocks the unsuspecting off their feet.

1	lemon wedge
	Superfine sugar to taste
1	shot Absolut Citron
1	teaspoon superfine sugar
1/2	shot Cointreau
1 1/2	shots fresh lemon juice

Rub the rim of a martini glass with the lemon wedge and dip in superfine sugar to taste. Combine the vodka, 1 teaspoon sugar, Cointreau, lemon juice and ice in a cocktail shaker and shake to mix. Strain into the prepared glass and garnish with a lemon twist.

For a festive touch, why not dip rims of glasses in tinted sugar for a pretty rainbow display? To tint sugar, just add 5 drops food coloring to 1 cup sugar. Mix well, let stand until dry and store in an airtight container until needed.

Serves 1

Old Town San Diego has the honor of being the oldest "civilized" area of California. Spanish missionaries settled here in 1769 and built the Presidio, the oldest California Catholic mission. Old Town is now a state park with lots of restaurants, many featuring the ubiquitous margarita. This particular League favorite is dedicated to Bill Kramer, the father of one of our most dedicated sustainers. We think you'll love it too.

old town margaritas

For those who like a sweeter margarita without sacrificing any of the zip.

SIMPLE SYRUP

1/4 cup sugar
1/4 cup water

MARGARITAS

1   cup tequila
1   cup fresh lime juice
1   cup Triple Sec
3/4 cup water

SYRUP   Heat the sugar and water in a saucepan until of a syrupy consistency, stirring frequently. Remove from the heat and let stand until cool.

MARGARITAS   Combine the syrup, tequila, lime juice, liqueur and water with ice in a blender. Process until the desired consistency. Pour into salt-rimmed margarita glasses and garnish with lime slices.

Serves 6 to 8

citrus margaritas

Vitamins for grown-ups.

1   cup orange-flavor liqueur
     (Cointreau)
1   cup tequila
1/4 cup fresh orange juice
1/4 cup fresh lime juice
1/4 cup fresh grapefruit juice
     Lime wedges
     Margarita salt

TIP   *If you're using a premium-brand tequila in this drink, be warned that salt will mask its expensive flavor, so serve these "naked."*

Combine the liqueur, tequila, orange juice, lime juice and grapefruit juice in a large pitcher and mix well. Chill, covered, in the refrigerator.

To serve, rub the rims of margarita glasses with lime wedges and dip in margarita salt, rotating gently to cover the rims evenly. Fill the salt-rimmed glasses with ice. Shake the chilled margarita mixture in a cocktail shaker filled with ice and strain into the prepared glasses. Garnish each serving with orange, lime and/or grapefruit slices.

Serves 8

old town margaritas

guacamole

We couldn't have a SoCal cookbook without this delicious regional staple!

1   avocado
1   Roma tomato, seeded and
      chopped
1   garlic clove, minced
      Juice of 1/2 lemon
1   small jalapeño chile, seeded
      and minced

Mash the avocado in a bowl. Stir in the tomato, garlic, lemon juice and jalapeño chile. Store, covered, in the refrigerator until serving time. Serve with tortilla chips.

Serves 2 to 4

TIP   *This recipe can easily be doubled or tripled. One avocado will serve two to four people. To keep this dish a pretty fresh green color, leave the pit in the serving bowl until the last minute.*

sun-dried tomato dip

Dip, dip, dip into this pretty treat. Paired with fresh vegetables, this is healthy happy hour heaven.

8   ounces reduced-fat cream
      cheese, cubed and softened
1/2   cup sour cream
1/2   cup light mayonnaise
1/4   cup drained oil-pack sun-dried
      tomatoes, chopped
1   teaspoon kosher salt
3/4   teaspoon freshly ground black
      pepper
10   dashes of hot red pepper sauce
2   scallions (white and green
      parts), thinly sliced

Combine the cream cheese, sour cream, mayonnaise, sun-dried tomatoes, salt, black pepper and pepper sauce in a food processor fitted with a metal blade. Process until mixed. Add the scallions and pulse 2 to 4 times or until combined. Serve at room temperature with assorted party crackers and/or vegetable crudités.

Serves 6 to 8

chile shrimp salsa with cayenne garlic bread

These look stunning served on a knobbly pottery platter. Warning: they disappear quickly!

SHRIMP SALSA

12 ounces chopped seeded red and/or yellow tomatoes (1 1/2 cups)
1/3 cup chopped fresh cilantro
1/3 cup fresh lime juice
1/3 cup olive oil
1/3 cup chopped red onion
2 tablespoons chopped fresh flat-leaf parsley
1 small serrano chile, seeded and minced
1 1/2 pounds large shrimp, cooked, peeled and deveined
Salt and pepper to taste

CAYENNE GARLIC BREAD

3/4 cup (1 1/2 sticks) butter, softened
6 garlic cloves, minced
1/4 teaspoon cayenne pepper
2 baguettes French bread

SALSA   Combine the tomatoes, cilantro, lime juice, olive oil, onion, parsley and serrano chile in a bowl and mix well. Let stand, covered, at room temperature for 1 hour. Cut the shrimp into quarters and add to the tomato mixture. Season with salt and pepper.

BREAD   Preheat the oven to 350 degrees. Mix the butter, garlic and cayenne pepper in a bowl until blended. Cut the baguettes into 1-inch slices and spread 1 side of each slice with some of the butter mixture. Wrap the baguettes in foil and bake for 20 minutes. To serve, spoon 1 tablespoon or more of the shrimp mixture on each baguette slice and arrange on a serving platter.

Serves 12

mushroom pâté

Not your typical veggie pâté. This dish is fresh, tasty, and keeps 'em coming back for more.

8	ounces fresh mushrooms, minced
2	tablespoons unsalted butter
1/4	cup minced green onion bulbs
1 1/2	teaspoons minced garlic
1/3	cup chicken stock
4	ounces reduced-fat cream cheese, softened
2	tablespoons unsalted butter, softened
2	tablespoons minced green onion tops
2	teaspoons Worcestershire sauce
2	teaspoons fresh lemon juice
1 1/2	teaspoons minced fresh thyme
1/2	teaspoon salt
	Freshly ground pepper to taste
	Chopped fresh parsley, bell pepper and/or green onions to taste

Sauté the mushrooms in 2 tablespoons butter in a medium skillet for 2 to 3 minutes. Stir in the minced green onion bulbs and garlic. Sauté for 1 minute. Add the stock and cook over high heat until all of the liquid is absorbed, stirring frequently. Remove from the heat and let stand until room temperature.

Mix the cream cheese and 2 tablespoons softened butter in a bowl until blended. Stir in the mushroom mixture, minced green onion tops, Worcestershire sauce, lemon juice, thyme, salt and pepper. Taste and adjust the seasonings.

Spoon the mushroom mixture into a 1-cup mold lined with plastic wrap. Chill until serving time. Invert the pâté onto a serving platter and sprinkle with parsley, bell pepper and/or additional green onions. Serve with toast points or assorted party crackers.

Serves 6

TIP *Instead of serving from a pâté mold, why not try showing this off in a pretty one-cup silver bowl?*

spicy crab-stuffed mushrooms

Serve a bunch of these mouth-watering treats as a great light lunch.

12 ounces white mushrooms, stems removed

1 pound lump crab meat, drained and shells and cartilage removed

4 ounces Pepper Jack cheese, shredded

2 ounces Parmesan cheese, grated

1 teaspoon chopped garlic

1 teaspoon Worcestershire sauce

1 teaspoon hot sauce

1/2 teaspoon salt

1/4 cup mayonnaise

2 ounces Parmesan cheese, grated

Preheat the oven to 350 degrees. Arrange the mushroom caps in a single layer on a baking sheet lined with baking parchment. Combine the crab meat, Pepper Jack cheese, 2 ounces Parmesan cheese, garlic, Worcestershire sauce, hot sauce and salt in a bowl and mix gently. Stir in the mayonnaise.

Mound a heaping tablespoon of the crab meat mixture into each mushroom cap and sprinkle with 2 ounces Parmesan cheese. Bake for 30 minutes. Serve warm.

Serves 8

marinated mushrooms

Great one-bite treats everyone will love.

2   pounds fresh white button
     mushrooms
     Salt to taste

1/2   cup olive oil

1/2   cup white wine vinegar

2   (or more) garlic cloves, crushed

1   teaspoon salt

1   teaspoon crushed oregano, or
     to taste

1/2   teaspoon chile pepper flakes,
     crushed

TIP   *The longer the mushrooms
marinate, the better the flavor.
Be sure to take them out of the
refrigerator in time for the olive
oil to come to room temperature.*

Trim a thin slice from the stem end of each mushroom. Drop the mushrooms into a saucepan of boiling salted water and reduce the heat.

Simmer for 5 minutes; do not boil. Drain the mushrooms and cover with cold water. Let stand until cool. Drain and pat dry with paper towels.

Whisk the olive oil, vinegar, garlic, 1 teaspoon salt, oregano and chile pepper flakes in a bowl. Add the mushrooms to the olive oil mixture and stir with a rubber spatula or wooden spoon until coated. Let stand at room temperature for 1 hour or longer, stirring occasionally.

Serves 12 to 15

Serrano chiles come from the Spanish word "serranias," meaning "foothills." The serrano chile is believed to have originated in the foothills of Puebla, Mexico. This tiny chile is hot, hot, hot, so handle with care. We advise wearing rubber gloves while handling and to peel and remove seeds under cold, running water. If gloves are not available, just coat your hands liberally with vegetable oil.

spicy shrimp cocktail

This twist on an old classic really turns up the heat. Serve with chilled beer, and enjoy!

2	cups tomato juice
1	cup bottled clam juice
1/2	cup sherry wine vinegar
20	large bunches cilantro, trimmed
2	serrano chiles, chopped
1	tablespoon Worcestershire sauce
2	pounds shrimp, peeled and deveined
1	tablespoon vegetable oil
1	large tomato, chopped
2	green onions, chopped
2	tablespoons chopped fresh cilantro
1	teaspoon lime juice
1	teaspoon sugar

Combine the tomato juice, clam juice, vinegar, 20 bunches cilantro, serrano chiles and Worcestershire sauce in a large saucepan. Bring to a boil and boil for 25 minutes or until the mixture is thickened and reduced to 1 2/3 cups, stirring occasionally. Strain into a bowl, discarding the solids.

Sauté the shrimp in the oil in a skillet for 2 minutes per side or until the shrimp turn pink. Combine the tomato, green onions, 2 tablespoons cilantro, lime juice and sugar in a bowl and mix well. Add the shrimp and clam juice mixture to the tomato mixture and mix well. Marinate, covered, in the refrigerator for 3 hours or longer. You may prepare up to 1 day in advance and store, covered, in the refrigerator.

Serves 4 to 6

lettuce wraps

Making these wraps serves as a great ice-breaker at a cocktail party.

1	tablespoon canola oil
2	tablespoons minced shallots
1	tablespoon minced garlic
1	tablespoon minced fresh gingerroot
1	pound ground pork or ground turkey
2	tablespoons soy sauce
1/4	cup sweet chili sauce
1	teaspoon fish sauce
1	teaspoon sugar
1/2	to 1 cup minced fresh cilantro leaves
4	sprigs of mint, stems removed (optional)
1/2	cup minced peanuts (optional)
1	head butter or Boston lettuce, separated

TIP   *Roll the lettuce leaf tightly and seal at both ends like a burrito to avoid messy fallout. This is finger food at its finest.*

Heat the canola oil in a wok or large skillet. Stir-fry the shallots in the hot oil for several minutes. Add the garlic and gingerroot and stir-fry for 1 minute. Add the ground pork and separate for even cooking. Stir in the soy sauce, chili sauce, fish sauce and sugar.

Cook until the ground pork is brown and crumbly and the liquid is reduced, stirring frequently. Stir in the cilantro. Spoon the ground pork mixture into a serving bowl. Place the mint sprigs and minced peanuts in small bowls and the lettuce on a platter. Instruct your guests to spoon some of the pork mixture onto a lettuce leaf and top with a couple of mint sprigs and minced peanuts and roll tightly.

Serves 4

lettuce wraps

teriyaki strips

Rich, delicious, and ultimately satisfying, these are protein snacks on a stick.

1/2 cup light soy sauce

1/4 cup California red table wine

1 garlic clove, crushed

2 tablespoons finely grated fresh gingerroot

2 tablespoons sugar, or to taste

1 pound top round steak, thinly sliced across the grain

TIP   *This recipe also works well with chicken or shellfish, but be aware that shellfish should not be marinated too long, or it will start to cook.*

Whisk the soy sauce, wine, garlic, gingerroot and sugar in a shallow dish. Add the steak and turn to coat. Marinate, covered, in the refrigerator for 2 to 10 hours, turning occasionally; drain. Soak 16 long bamboo skewers in water to cover for 30 minutes.

Preheat the broiler. Thread the steak strips on the skewers and arrange the skewers on a broiler rack lined with foil. Broil for 5 minutes per side or to the desired degree of doneness. Arrange the skewers on a serving platter and garnish with sprigs of parsley. You may prepare in advance, store in the refrigerator and reheat in the microwave just before serving.

Serves 16

roasted vegetable tart

A guilt-free happy hour treat. What more could you want?

1   eggplant, cut into 1/4-inch slices
2   portobello mushrooms, sliced
1   red bell pepper, cut into
     1/2-inch slices
1   zucchini, cut into 1/4-inch slices
2   tablespoons olive oil
     Salt and pepper to taste
4   ounces Roquefort or other blue
     cheese, crumbled
3   ounces cream cheese, softened
1   egg
1   tablespoon grated Parmesan
     cheese
2   refrigerator pie pastries

Preheat the oven to 450 degrees. Toss the eggplant, mushrooms, bell pepper and zucchini with the olive oil in a large roasting pan. Season with salt and pepper. Roast for 12 to 14 minutes or until the vegetables are tender, stirring once or twice. Beat the Roquefort cheese and cream cheese in a mixing bowl until smooth. Add the egg and Parmesan cheese and beat until blended.

Unfold each pie pastry on a baking sheet and pinch any tears. Spread 1/2 of the cheese mixture to within 2 inches of the edge over each pastry. Arrange the roasted vegetables evenly over the cheese and fold the pastry over, partially covering the filling. Bake for 15 to 20 minutes or until the pastry is brown. Cut into wedges.

Serves 8 to 10

Whether you're serving up a gourmet fantasy or just eating at the kitchen table, having a dinner party in is one of the best nights out.

dinner

We'd like to take a moment to talk about a true California phenomenon: what we call the "mañana philosophy." Out here, relaxed and sun-dazed, it's easy to let the days slip by like pretty beads on a string, carrying one thing over to the next, to the next, to the next…or, as we like to call it, waiting until mañana. But while this may apply to finishing work on the house or starting that hot new exercise class, there's one thing we've found that our family never wants to wait on: dinner.

Dinner is the centerpoint to the day, the time when we come together and sit down to be with one another in a special way. It is communion in more ways than one—the traditional dinner nourishes more than just our bodies; it holds the fabric of our family together. Of course, that doesn't mean that every night has to be an all-singing, all-dancing mom's-the-greatest four-course extravaganza. We do live in the real world, after all. But great choices like our Wild Mushroom Risotto; Penne with Sausage and Asparagus; or Never-Fail Pesto will delight everyone without leaving you feeling like Little Orphan Annie in the kitchen with nothing but a stack of dripping dishes to keep you company.

And as for the dinner party? Well, there's no better opportunity to dress yourself up a bit—even if out here that means pairing a killer pair of strappy sandals with faded jeans—and show yourself off, surrounded by good friends, good food, and good wine. (By the way, we've found that the best way to get the guys to bond is to let them do the dishes together. Trust us: it's a social service!). Whether you're serving up a gourmet fantasy or just eating at the kitchen table, having a dinner party in is one of the best nights out that we know of.

dinner menus

president's dinner

If there's one thing we Junior Leaguers know, it's hospitality. From a one-hour meeting to a weekend retreat, who's hosting the food and drinks is always an important agenda item with us! For the JLSD, our president sets the standards—typically, the incoming president hosts a dinner in her home for the new Board of Directors. This provides the group with a warm welcome, while gearing up to do some serious work over the coming year. We think this is the perfect menu for this occasion— why not try it at your League?

appetizers
lettuce wraps (Happy Hour, p. 122)
   fresh vegetables
with red pepper coulis
   mushroom pâté (Happy Hour, p. 118)
sliced crusty french baguettes

dinner
mediterranean couscous
   with roasted vegetables (Lunch, p. 74)
sautéed chicken breasts with
   artichokes and olives

dessert
molten chocolate cakes
   with fresh berries and vanilla
ice cream (Dessert, p. 177)

dinner on the deck

socal mojitos (Happy Hour, p. 112)
grilled avocado and tomato salad
swordfish with tomatillo salsa
jalapeño corn muffins
california pear pie (Dessert, p. 170)

Casual, yes. Impressive—oh, yes. This is a good, easy dinner for you to prepare, and one that will seriously raise your status with guests. Get the guys to man the grill, and you should have plenty of time to enjoy a Mojito yourself.

elegant occasion

lemon drop martini (Happy Hour, p. 113)
sun-dried tomato and goat cheese bruschetta (Midnight Snack, p. 192)
tomato salad with capers and olives
garlic scallops
chocolate macadamia torte (Dessert, p. 178)

When the in-laws are in town, this is the menu to make. Strong, clean flavors are the stars of this show, and these pairings make a really beautiful plate. Polish up your silver and your small talk and go forth, sure that this is a winner.

simply san diego

old town margaritas (Happy Hour, p. 114)
cheese soufflé with corn and jalapeños
grilled pork tenderloin with tortillas and guacamole
margarita cake (Dessert, p. 184)

This may be the most representational dinner of who we are—but these courses would be equally as delicious in Detroit, Dallas...wherever good cooks like to ply their trade. For grown-up Mexican-American flair, this menu can't be beat.

black bean salsa

What California cookbook could be without it?

2	(15-ounce) cans black beans
	Juice of 1 lime
2	tablespoons red wine vinegar
1	tablespoon balsamic vinegar
2	tablespoons sugar
1/2	teaspoon salt
1	mango, cut into 1/2-inch pieces
2/3	cup finely chopped green bell pepper
1/2	cup finely chopped red onion
1	jalapeño chile, finely chopped (optional)
1	tablespoon safflower oil
1	garlic clove, crushed
	Freshly ground pepper to taste

Drain the beans and rinse under cold water for 1 minute. Combine the lime juice, wine vinegar and balsamic vinegar in a bowl and mix well. Add the sugar and salt and stir until dissolved. Add the beans, mango, bell pepper, onion, jalapeño chile, safflower oil, garlic and pepper and stir gently. Chill, covered, for 24 hours. Serve with baked tortilla chips. For variety, serve as a side salad with fish or chicken or over hot cooked rice as a quick low-fat meal. You may substitute a mixture of 1/3 cup chopped red bell pepper and 1/3 cup chopped green bell pepper for 2/3 cup chopped green bell pepper.

Baked pita chips also make good scoopers. Split pita rounds into halves and cut into wedges with kitchen shears. Toast in the oven for about 3 minutes or until crisp.

Serves 10 to 12

knock-your-socks-off hot crab dip

Of course there is a hot crab dip recipe. . .and this one is really great.

4	ounces cream cheese, cubed
1/2	cup dry white wine
1	(16-ounce) can water-pack artichoke hearts, drained and finely chopped
1	pound fresh crab meat, drained and shells removed
1	cup mayonnaise
2	ounces blue cheese, finely crumbled
1	egg, beaten

Preheat the oven to 350 degrees. Combine the cream cheese and wine in a saucepan. Cook over low heat until the cheese is creamy, stirring frequently. Remove from the heat and whisk until blended. Fold in the artichokes, crab meat, mayonnaise, blue cheese and egg. Spoon the crab meat mixture into an 8×8-inch baking dish. Bake for 30 minutes and garnish with sliced black olives. Serve warm with assorted party crackers. You may substitute two drained 8-ounce cans crab meat for the fresh crab meat.

Makes 4 cups

spinach soup

Like a funnel of delicious vitamins...virtue and reward all in one!

2   tablespoons clarified butter
3   cups chopped onions
3   cups chicken stock
1 1/2 pounds fresh spinach, or
      2 (10-ounce) packages frozen
      spinach, thawed
3   tablespoons butter
2   tablespoons unbleached
      white flour
3   cups milk
1 1/2 teaspoons salt
1   teaspoon freshly ground pepper
1/2   teaspoon freshly grated nutmeg

Melt the clarified butter in a heavy saucepan. Cook the onions in the butter over low heat until tender, stirring frequently; do not brown. Add the stock and bring to a boil. Reduce the heat to low.

Simmer for 10 minutes. Reserve a few of the perfect spinach leaves for garnish and add the remaining spinach to the stock mixture. Return to a boil and remove from the heat. Let stand until cool.

Heat the butter in a heavy saucepan until melted. Stir in the flour. Cook for 2 minutes, stirring constantly. Add the milk gradually, stirring constantly. Cook until the mixture begins to boil, stirring frequently. Remove from the heat.

Process the spinach mixture in a food processor fitted with a metal blade until puréed. Add the purée, salt, pepper and nutmeg to the milk mixture and mix well. Simmer just until heated through, stirring occasionally; do not boil. Ladle into soup bowls and garnish with the reserved spinach leaves.

Serves 6

lobster bisque

Really, truly worth the work.

1/2 carrot, finely chopped
1 1/2 ribs celery, finely chopped
1/4 white onion, finely chopped
1 1/2 tablespoons brandy
2 1/2 cups heavy cream
1 1/2 cups milk
1 cup lobster stock (reduced to 2 ounces), or 1 1/2 ounces lobster base
3 ounces shrimp, peeled and finely chopped
3 ounces lobster meat, chopped
3 tablespoons butter
1/3 cup flour
1 1/2 tablespoons paprika
1/4 teaspoon cayenne pepper

Sauté the carrot, celery and onion in a large nonstick saucepan until tender-crisp. Stir in the brandy and cook for 2 minutes, stirring occasionally. Add the heavy cream, milk, stock, shrimp and lobster meat. Bring to a simmer and cook until the shrimp and lobster are cooked through.

Heat the butter in a skillet until melted. Stir in the flour and cook until thickened and bubbly, stirring constantly. Stir in the paprika and cayenne pepper. Add the roux to the lobster mixture gradually, whisking constantly. Bring to a simmer and ladle into soup bowls.

Serves 6

avocado and tomato salad

We just plain love this. It's what California is all about!

DIJON BALSAMIC VINAIGRETTE

6	tablespoons olive oil
2	tablespoons balsamic vinegar
1	teaspoon mild Dijon mustard
1	garlic clove, finely chopped
1/2	teaspoon salt
	Freshly ground pepper to taste

SALAD

1	small Haas avocado, chopped
3	Roma tomatoes or small vine-ripened tomatoes, chopped
1/2	cup dried cranberries
1/4	cup pine nuts, toasted
1 1/2	to 2 ounces goat cheese, crumbled
1	head butter, red leaf or green leaf lettuce, torn and chilled
	Freshly ground pepper to taste

VINAIGRETTE   Combine the olive oil, vinegar, mustard, garlic, salt and pepper in a jar with a tight-fitting lid and seal tightly. Shake to mix.

SALAD   Toss the avocado, tomatoes, cranberries, pine nuts and goat cheese with 1/4 cup of the vinaigrette in a salad bowl. Let stand for 10 minutes. Add the lettuce to the avocado mixture and toss to coat. Divide the salad evenly among 4 serving plates and sprinkle with pepper. Serve immediately.

Serves 4

grilled avocado and tomato salad

Great texture, great taste, great for you.

3   tablespoons fresh lemon juice
    (about 2 lemons)
2   ripe firm large avocados
1/2 red onion, thinly sliced and
    separated into rings
    Salt and freshly ground pepper
    to taste
1   pound vine-ripened tomatoes
2   tablespoons extra-virgin olive oil
4   teaspoons Never-Fail Pesto
    (page 147)
    Freshly grated Parmesan cheese
    to taste
1   tablespoon pine nuts, lightly
    toasted (optional)

Preheat the grill to medium. Pour the lemon juice into a nonreactive bowl large enough to hold the avocados in a single layer. Cut the avocados into halves and remove the pits. Scoop out the flesh in 1 piece with a spoon. Immediately toss the avocados with the lemon juice to prevent discoloration.

Place the onion in a bowl. Pour some of the lemon juice from the avocados over the onion and season with salt and pepper. Toss to coat. Cut the tomatoes into thin wedges and season with salt and pepper.

Remove the avocados from the lemon juice using a slotted spoon, reserving the juice and bowl. Sprinkle the avocados with salt and pepper and drizzle with 1 tablespoon of the olive oil. Arrange the avocados cut side down on the grill rack. Grill for 2 minutes or until the outside edges appear dry and brown; turn. Grill for 2 minutes longer. If the avocados are very firm, continue grilling for 1 minute longer to soften. Return the grilled avocados to the bowl containing the lemon juice and turn to coat. Cool and cut into thin wedges.

To serve, arrange the onion rings evenly in the center of 4 salad plates. Place the avocado slices on opposite sides of the plates and then arrange the tomato slices on the remaining opposite sides. Drizzle each salad with 3/4 teaspoon of the remaining olive oil and 1 teaspoon of the pesto. Sprinkle with salt, pepper, cheese and pine nuts. Serve immediately.

Serves 4

warm goat cheese salad

Finally, a good, dependable recipe for a beloved restaurant classic.

DIJON VINAIGRETTE

1/4   cup extra-virgin olive oil
2   garlic cloves, cut into halves
2   tablespoons Dijon mustard
2   tablespoons red wine vinegar
1   tablespoon chopped fresh basil
      Salt and pepper to taste

SALAD

1   cup panko
1   tablespoon chopped fresh
      thyme
1   tablespoon chopped fresh
      parsley
1   tablespoon chopped fresh basil
1/2   teaspoon ground pepper
1/4   teaspoon salt
3   (4-ounce) logs soft fresh goat
      cheese
2   egg whites, lightly beaten
1   tablespoon olive oil
10   ounces mixed baby
      salad greens
      Salt and pepper to taste

TIP   *Panko, Japanese bread crumbs,
are available at Asian markets and
in the Asian food section of some
supermarkets. If panko is unavailable,
substitute plain bread crumbs. It
won't have the same wonderful
texture, but it will do the trick.*

VINAIGRETTE   Combine the olive oil and garlic in a small microwave-safe cup and cover tightly with plastic wrap. Microwave for 30 seconds. Remove the garlic to a bowl, reserving the oil. Coarsely mash the garlic with a fork. Add the mustard, vinegar and basil to the garlic and mix until smooth. Add the reserved oil gradually, whisking constantly until blended. Season with salt and pepper. You may prepare up to 1 day in advance and store, covered, in the refrigerator. Bring to room temperature before serving.

SALAD   Mix the panko, thyme, parsley, basil, pepper and 1/4 teaspoon salt in a bowl. Cut each cheese log crosswise into halves and flatten each half into a 1/2-inch-thick round. Dip each round in the egg whites and coat with the panko mixture. Arrange on a plate and chill, covered, for 1 to 8 hours.

Heat the olive oil in a large nonstick skillet over medium-high heat. Cook the cheese rounds in the hot oil for 3 minutes per side or until golden brown and crisp; drain. Toss the salad greens in a bowl with the vinaigrette until coated. Season with salt and pepper to taste. Divide the salad greens equally among 6 serving plates. Top each with 1 cheese round and serve immediately.

Serves 6

holiday salad

A fun side dish to lighten up the holiday season—or any time at all.

POPPY SEED DRESSING

2/3	cup vegetable oil
1/2	cup sugar
1/3	cup lemon juice
1	tablespoon poppy seeds
2	teaspoons chopped onion
1	teaspoon Dijon mustard
1/2	teaspoon salt

SALAD

1	head romaine, torn or cut into bite-size pieces
	Grated Parmesan cheese to taste
	Dried cranberries to taste
	Cashews or pistachios to taste
1	apple, chopped
1	pear, chopped

DRESSING   Combine the oil, sugar, lemon juice, poppy seeds, onion, mustard and salt in a jar with a tight-fitting lid and seal tightly. Shake to mix.

SALAD   Mix the romaine, cheese, cranberries, cashews, apple and pear in a salad bowl. Add the desired amount of dressing and toss to coat. Serve immediately.

Serves 6 to 8

tomato salad with capers and olives

Strong, clean flavors and a beautiful presentation make this salad hard to beat.

6	large tomatoes, sliced
2	tablespoons balsamic vinegar
5	tablespoons olive oil
	Salt and pepper to taste
1/3	cup pitted kalamata olives
1/3	cup crumbled blue cheese
2	tablespoons drained capers

Arrange the tomatoes on a large platter. Drizzle with the vinegar and then with the olive oil. Sprinkle lightly with salt and generously with pepper. Top with the olives, blue cheese and capers. Garnish with fresh basil and serve immediately.

Serves 6

heirloom tomato salad with tapenade and chèvre toasts

This is seriously fabulous. Your guests will be in dining heaven.

TAPENADE
2   cups pitted kalamata or niçoise olives
2   tablespoons capers
1   bunch basil, finely chopped
2   anchovy fillets, finely chopped
2   tablespoons almonds, toasted and finely chopped
1   garlic clove, finely chopped
1   teaspoon grated orange zest
1/2   cup extra-virgin olive oil
    Freshly ground pepper to taste

TOASTS
1   baguette
1/4   cup (or more) olive oil

VINAIGRETTE
2   tablespoons red wine vinegar
1   shallot, minced
1   garlic clove, crushed
1/2   cup extra-virgin olive oil
1/16   teaspoon salt

SALAD AND ASSEMBLY
2   pounds heirloom tomatoes (various colors and sizes)
1/2   pint assorted cherry tomatoes
    Salt and pepper to taste
1/2   cup fresh herbs (mixture of basil, marjoram, thyme, Italian parsley or oregano), chopped
4   ounces chèvre

TAPENADE   Rinse the olives and capers, pat dry and finely chop. Combine the olives, capers, basil, anchovies, almonds, garlic and orange zest in a bowl and mix well. Add the olive oil and stir until combined. Season with pepper. Taste and adjust the seasonings.

TOASTS   Preheat the oven to 400 degrees. Cut the baguette into twenty-four 1/4-inch slices with a serrated knife. Brush each side lightly with the olive oil and arrange in a single layer on a baking sheet. Bake until light brown on both sides. Remove to a wire rack to cool.

VINAIGRETTE   Combine the vinegar, shallot and garlic in a nonreactive bowl. Let sit for at least 10 minutes. Whisk in the olive oil and salt. Taste and adjust the flavor with additional vinegar and/or olive oil if needed.

SALAD   Core the larger heirloom tomatoes and cut into slices or wedges. Cut the cherry tomatoes into halves.

ASSEMBLY   Divide the tomatoes evenly among 6 plates or arrange on a large serving platter. Sprinkle with salt, pepper and herbs. Drizzle with the desired amount of vinaigrette. Spread the tapenade on half of the toasts and spread the chèvre on the remaining toasts. Arrange 2 tapenade toasts and 2 chèvre toasts on each plate. Serve immediately.

Serves 6

black bean and barley salad

You're really going to thank us for this one, and so will the family.

3 tablespoons olive oil
2 tablespoons orange juice
2 tablespoons rice wine vinegar
1 garlic clove, minced
1/2 teaspoon cumin
1/4 teaspoon cayenne pepper
1/2 cup sliced green onions
2/3 cup barley
  Chicken broth
1 (16-ounce) can black beans, drained and rinsed
2 tomatoes, seeded and chopped
1/2 cup chopped celery

TIP   *A great substitute for salsa and very popular with men.*

Combine the olive oil, orange juice, vinegar, garlic, cumin, cayenne pepper and green onions in a bowl and mix well. Cook the barley in a saucepan using the package directions and substituting chicken broth for the liquid. Let stand until cool.

Mix the barley, beans, tomatoes and celery in a bowl. Add the olive oil mixture to the barley mixture and mix until combined. Chill, covered, until serving time.

Serves 4

asparagus with red pepper confetti

This is so pretty, and a fun alternative to a butter sauce.

2 pounds asparagus spears
1 red bell pepper, cut into thin strips
2 tablespoons olive oil
1/4 cup fresh lemon juice
1/2 cup chopped fresh dill weed
Freshly ground pepper to taste

TIP *Asparagus is best cooked the same day it is purchased but will keep, sealed tightly in a plastic bag, for three to four days in the refrigerator.*

Preheat the oven to 350 degrees. Snap off the woody ends of the asparagus spears and discard. Arrange the asparagus in a single layer on a sheet of foil large enough to fold over and seal. Transfer the foil and contents to a baking dish for support.

Layer the bell pepper strips over the asparagus and drizzle with the olive oil and lemon juice. Sprinkle with the dill weed and pepper. Fold the foil over the asparagus mixture to cover and seal the edges (snugly but not tightly). Bake for 10 to 15 minutes or to the desired degree of doneness. Serve immediately. You may prepare in advance and bake just before serving.

Serves 8

red pepper coulis

Pure summer goodness, good all year round.

1 tablespoon butter
1/2 small onion, finely chopped
2 large red bell peppers, chopped
Freshly ground pepper to taste
1 cup chicken broth
3 tablespoons extra-virgin olive oil

TIP *Coulis is a fine accompaniment to striped bass or swordfish, and it also makes a great dipping sauce for firm vegetables. Try pairing with prosciutto-wrapped asparagus—yum!*

Heat the butter in a saucepan. Add the onion to the butter and cook until glazed, stirring frequently. Stir in the bell peppers and season with pepper. Add the broth and bring to a boil, stirring frequently with a wooden spoon to dislodge any browned bits. Reduce the heat to low.

Simmer for 15 to 20 minutes, stirring occasionally. Remove from the heat. Process the bell pepper mixture in a blender until puréed. Return the purée to the saucepan and simmer for 5 minutes or until the consistency of heavy cream, stirring occasionally. Stir in the olive oil.

Serves 4

cheese soufflé with corn and jalapeños

This is so yummy, we have seen guests picking the brown bits off the serving dish to eat when it's all gone.

2   onions, sliced
2   tablespoons unsalted butter
2   fresh jalapeño chiles, cut into
         halves lengthwise, seeded and
         cut into strips
2   garlic cloves, minced
1 1/2 cups fresh corn kernels
         Salt and freshly ground pepper
         to taste
2   tablespoons unsalted butter
1 1/4 cups (5 ounces) shredded
         Monterey Jack cheese
2/3   cup shredded sharp Cheddar
         cheese
6   extra-large eggs, lightly beaten
1/2   cup milk

Preheat the oven to 350 degrees. Cook the onions in 2 tablespoons butter in an ovenproof 10-inch nonstick skillet over low heat until tender but not brown. Stir in the jalapeño chiles and garlic. Cook for 2 minutes, stirring constantly. Add the corn, salt and pepper and mix well. Cook for 1 minute, stirring frequently.

Spoon 2/3 of the corn mixture into a bowl. Stir 2 tablespoons butter into the remaining corn mixture. Toss the Monterey Jack cheese and Cheddar cheese in a bowl. Sprinkle 1/3 of the cheese mixture over the corn mixture in the skillet and spread with 1/2 of the corn mixture in the bowl. Sprinkle with 1/2 of the remaining cheese mixture and top with the remaining corn mixture in the bowl.

Whisk the eggs, milk, salt and pepper in a bowl until blended and pour over the prepared layers. Sprinkle with the remaining cheese mixture. Bake for 25 minutes or until puffed and brown. Serve hot or at room temperature.

Serves 4 to 6

tomato provençal

Fabulous for an elegant dinner for two or a straight-from-the-oven family affair.

2   tomatoes
     Salt and freshly ground pepper
     to taste

2   tablespoons chopped
     fresh thyme

1   tablespoon chopped fresh
     rosemary

$1/2$ bunch parsley, trimmed

1   shallot

$1/2$ garlic clove

$1/2$ cup bread crumbs

2   tablespoons olive oil

Preheat the oven to 375 degrees. Cut the tomatoes horizontally into halves and trim the ends to allow the tomatoes to stand upright. Sprinkle with salt and pepper.

Combine the thyme, rosemary, parsley, shallot and garlic in a food processor fitted with a steel blade. Process until chopped. Stir in the bread crumbs and 1 tablespoon of the olive oil. Mound the bread crumb mixture on the cut sides of the tomatoes.

Brush the bottom of a baking dish with the remaining 1 tablespoon olive oil and arrange the tomato halves bread crumb side up in the dish. Bake for 20 minutes. You may substitute about $1 1/2$ to 2 cups loosely packed chopped spinach for the parsley or a combination of spinach and parsley for the parsley if desired.

Serves 4

jalapeño corn muffins

Like your mother's corn bread—only better, with a real pow-wow kick.

1   cup flour
1   cup stone-ground cornmeal
1   teaspoon salt
1   teaspoon baking soda
2   or 3 ears of fresh corn
3   small jalapeño chiles, seeded and minced
14   tablespoons unsalted butter
2   teaspoons chopped fresh rosemary
2   tablespoons brown sugar
1   egg
$1^1/4$ cups buttermilk

TIP   *Wear gloves when chopping jalapeño chiles, and do not touch your eyes! If gloves are not available, rub your hands liberally with vegetable oil.*

Preheat the oven to 425 degrees. Mix the flour, cornmeal, salt and baking soda together. Cut the tops of the corn kernels into a bowl using a sharp knife. Cook the jalapeño chiles in 1 tablespoon of the butter in a saucepan over low heat for 1 minute. Remove from the heat and stir in the corn and rosemary.

Beat the remaining 13 tablespoons butter and brown sugar in a mixing bowl until creamy. Add the egg and beat until light and fluffy, scraping the bowl occasionally. Add the flour mixture and buttermilk alternately 1/4 at a time, beating well after each addition. Stir in the jalapeño chile mixture.

Spoon the batter into muffin cups sprayed with nonstick cooking spray or coated with additional butter. Bake for 18 to 20 minutes or until light brown. Cool in the pan for 5 minutes. Serve warm.

Makes 1 dozen muffins

jalapeño corn muffins

wild mushroom risotto

Much easier than the old "stand there and keep stirring" risotto, and it tastes great too.

3	cups vegetable broth
1	cup red wine
8	ounces portobello mushrooms, chopped
2	tablespoons butter
1	cup medium grain white rice or arborio rice
2	tablespoons chopped fresh thyme, or 1 tablespoon dried thyme
1/4	cup (1 ounce) grated Parmesan cheese

Bring the broth and wine to a simmer in a small saucepan. Remove from the heat. Cover to keep warm.

Sauté the mushrooms in the butter in a saucepan over medium-high heat until the mushrooms are tender and begin to release their juices. Stir in the rice, 1 tablespoon of the thyme and all but 1/4 cup of the warm broth mixture. Reduce the heat to medium.

Simmer for 20 minutes or until the rice is almost tender, stirring occasionally. Stir in the remaining 1/4 cup broth mixture. Cook for a few more minutes or until the rice is tender and the mixture is creamy, stirring occasionally. Remove from the heat and stir in the remaining tablespoon thyme and cheese. Serve as a side dish or with a salad and bread for a light meal.

Serves 4

fusilli with mushrooms and arugula

Who needs spaghetti?

1/3 cup sun-dried tomatoes (not oil pack)

3 tablespoons boiling water

1 1/2 tablespoons balsamic vinegar

1 1/2 teaspoons sugar

1 teaspoon finely chopped fresh marjoram

12 ounces fusilli

1/4 cup virgin olive oil

4 cups chopped domestic or wild mushrooms
Salt and freshly ground pepper to taste

1 1/2 tablespoons minced garlic

1/2 cup loosely packed fresh basil leaves

2 cups canned Roma tomatoes, chopped

3/4 cup (3 ounces) freshly grated Parmigiano-Reggiano cheese

4 cups fresh arugula

2 tablespoons pine nuts, lightly toasted
Red pepper flakes (optional)

Combine the sun-dried tomatoes, boiling water, vinegar, sugar and marjoram in a heatproof bowl and mix well. Let stand for 10 minutes or until rehydrated; drain. Cut the tomatoes into julienne strips. Cook the pasta in boiling water in a saucepan for 10 minutes or until al dente. Drain, reserving 1/2 cup of the cooking liquid.

Heat the olive oil in a large sauté pan over medium-high heat until hot. Sauté the mushrooms in the hot oil for 1 minute; do not stir. Stir and sauté for 5 minutes longer or until the mushrooms are brown on all sides. Season with salt and pepper. Stir in the garlic and sauté until the garlic is light brown. Add the basil and julienned sun-dried tomatoes and mix well. Cook for several minutes, stirring frequently. Stir in the Roma tomatoes and bring to a simmer. Fold in the pasta, 1/2 cup of the cheese and the reserved cooking liquid. Add 3 cups of the arugula and toss until barely wilted.

Spoon the pasta mixture into a bowl or onto a serving platter and top with the remaining 1 cup arugula. Sprinkle with the pine nuts, some of the remaining 1/4 cup cheese and red pepper flakes. Serve with the remaining cheese.

Serves 4

sun-dried tomato pasta

A great Sunday-night staple, and so quick and easy to prepare.

16 ounces rotini
3   cups broccoli crowns
2   cups sliced mushrooms
1/2 cup olive oil
1/3 cup white wine vinegar
2   tablespoons minced garlic
3/4 cup oil-pack sun-dried tomatoes, chopped
2/3 cup freshly grated Parmesan cheese

Cook the pasta using the package directions; drain. Cover to keep warm. Combine the broccoli, mushrooms, olive oil, vinegar and garlic in a large saucepan and mix well. Simmer over low heat for 5 minutes or until the broccoli is tender-crisp, stirring occasionally. Stir in the sun-dried tomatoes.

Simmer for 5 minutes longer, stirring occasionally. Remove from the heat. Fold in the pasta. Spoon the pasta mixture into a serving bowl and sprinkle with the cheese. Serve warm.

Serves 6 to 8

never-fail pesto

We can't think of any occasion when we would not love to eat this.

2 cups firmly packed fresh
basil leaves

1/2 cup virgin olive oil

1/3 cup pine nuts, lightly toasted

3 garlic cloves, chopped

1/2 teaspoon salt
Freshly ground pepper to taste

3/4 cup (3 ounces) grated
Parmigiano-Reggiano cheese

2 tablespoons unsalted butter,
softened

Combine the basil, olive oil, pine nuts, garlic, salt and pepper in a blender or food processor. Process until smooth, scraping the side once or twice with a rubber spatula. Add the cheese and butter and process for 15 seconds. Scrape the side again and process for a few more seconds. Do not overprocess, as the texture of a good pesto is always a little chunky.

To chill or freeze, process all of the ingredients except the cheese and butter. Store in a jar with a tight-fitting lid in the refrigerator, or freeze in a freezer container. To prevent a dark layer from forming on the top, drizzle additional olive oil on the surface or place a sheet of plastic wrap on top of the pesto before sealing. To serve, allow the pesto to come to room temperature and beat in the cheese and butter.

Makes enough sauce for 1 pound pasta

penne with sausage and asparagus

This is as delicious as it is pretty.

1 1/2 cups finely chopped onions
6   garlic cloves, finely chopped
2   tablespoons olive oil
2   red bell peppers, chopped
2   yellow bell peppers, chopped
2   pounds turkey or Italian sausage
1   cup white wine
1   (28-ounce) can Italian plum
      tomatoes
1   tablespoon chopped fresh
      oregano
1/4   teaspoon black pepper
1/4   teaspoon crushed red
      pepper flakes
1   pound asparagus, trimmed and
      diagonally sliced
1 1/2 pounds penne, cooked and
      drained
      Freshly grated Parmigiano-
      Reggiano cheese

Sauté the onions and garlic in the olive oil in a medium saucepan until the onions are tender. Stir in the bell peppers. Sauté for 5 to 10 minutes longer or until the bell peppers are tender.

Cook the sausage 1 pound at a time in a large skillet for 25 minutes or until brown on all sides. Drain on paper towels, reserving 1 tablespoon of the pan drippings. Cut the sausage into 1/4-inch slices.

Heat the reserved pan drippings over medium heat. Add the wine and stir to dislodge any browned bits. Stir in the onion mixture, sausage, undrained tomatoes, oregano, black pepper and red pepper. Simmer for 15 minutes, stirring occasionally. Add the asparagus and cook for 10 minutes longer or until the asparagus is tender, stirring occasionally. Fold in the pasta. Spoon the pasta mixture into a serving bowl and sprinkle with cheese.

Serves 8 to 10

penne with sausage and asparagus

grilled halibut with pineapple mango salsa

Welcome to the Pacific Rim. . .come on in, the water's warm.

TROPICAL SALSA

1	cup chunks fresh pineapple
3/4	cup chunks fresh mango
2/3	cup chunks fresh papaya
1/2	cup chunks seeded tomato
1/3	cup chunks seeded cucumber
1/3	cup chunks red onion
3	tablespoons minced fresh cilantro
2	tablespoons minced fresh mint
2	tablespoons minced seeded jalapeño chile
2	tablespoons fresh lime juice
	Salt to taste

HALIBUT

6	(6-ounce) halibut fillets, or any firm white fish
	Olive oil
	Salt and pepper to taste

TIP *For a fun presentation, save the top of the pineapple and place in the middle of the serving platter. Arrange the grilled fillets facing away from the pineapple top, and pour the Tropical Salsa around the inside area of the platter and on top of the fillets.*

SALSA   Combine the pineapple, mango, papaya, tomato, cucumber, onion, cilantro, mint, jalapeño chile and lime juice in a bowl and mix well. Season with salt. Chill, covered, for 1 to 4 hours, stirring occasionally.

HALIBUT   Preheat the grill to medium-high. Brush the fillets with olive oil and sprinkle with salt and pepper. Grill over hot coals for about 5 minutes per side or just until the fillets are opaque in the center. Arrange 1 fillet on each of 6 dinner plates and top each with some of the salsa. Serve immediately. To prevent the fillets from sticking to the grill rack, place the fillets in a grill basket coated with nonstick cooking spray before placing on the grill rack.

Serves 6

grilled salmon with spinach and yogurt dill sauce

After trying this, we're so over poached salmon.

YOGURT DILL SAUCE

1/2 cup nonfat yogurt

2 tablespoons prepared horseradish

1 teaspoon minced fresh dill weed

SALMON

4 (2 1/2-ounce) salmon fillets

SPINACH AND ASSEMBLY

1/4 cup white wine

2 teaspoons minced garlic

10 ounces fresh spinach leaves, trimmed, or 1 (10-ounce) package frozen spinach, thawed

1/16 teaspoon freshly grated nutmeg

1/16 teaspoon freshly ground pepper

TIP   *For perfectly cooked fish every time, measure the thickest part of the cut and cook, any way, for 10 minutes per inch of thickness.*

SAUCE   Whisk the yogurt, horseradish and dill weed in a bowl until combined.

SALMON   Preheat the grill and spray the hot grill rack with nonstick cooking spray. Grill the salmon over hot coals for 2 minutes per side, turning to make diamond or square grill marks for presentation. Remove the salmon to a platter and cover to keep warm.

SPINACH   Heat the wine in a large sauté pan over medium-low heat. Sauté the garlic in the hot wine for 1 minute. Add the spinach to the garlic mixture and sauté just until the spinach turns bright green and wilts. (If the garlic sticks to the pan, add 1 to 2 tablespoons vegetable broth or water.) Sprinkle the spinach with the nutmeg and pepper.

ASSEMBLY   Pat the spinach dry and portion evenly on 4 heated serving plates. Arrange the salmon so as to partially cover the spinach and drizzle with the sauce. Garnish each plate with 1 sprig of dill weed and 1 lemon wedge.

Serves 4

swordfish with tomatillo salsa

A really tasty swordfish recipe.

TOMATILLO SALSA

6	fresh tomatillos
1	small red onion, cut into chunks
2	garlic cloves, chopped
1	large fresh Anaheim chile or other mild green chile, seeded and chopped
1/2	fresh red or green jalapeño chile, seeded and chopped
1/4	cup cilantro sprigs
	Salt to taste

SWORDFISH

4	(6- to 8-ounce) swordfish steaks, 1 inch thick
2	tablespoons vegetable oil
	Salt and freshly ground pepper to taste

TIP   *To serve this dinner with style, decorate plates with crushed red and blue corn tortilla chips.*

SALSA   Discard the papery husks from the tomatillos and chop coarsely. Combine the tomatillos, onion, garlic, Anaheim chile, jalapeño chile and cilantro in a food processor. Process just until coarsely chopped. Spoon into a bowl and season with salt.

SWORDFISH   Preheat the grill. Position the oiled grill rack 4 to 6 inches above the heat source. Rub the steaks with the oil and sprinkle with salt and pepper.

Grill for 10 minutes or until the steaks have turned from translucent to opaque throughout, turning once or twice. Remove the steaks to a heated platter and top each with a spoonful of the salsa. Serve with the remaining salsa.

Serves 4

swordfish with tomatillo salsa

garlic scallops

So great—but make your date eat some too, or you might be going home alone.

8   scallops with roe
     Sea salt and pepper to taste
3   tablespoons olive oil
1/4 cup (1/2 stick) butter
3   garlic cloves, finely chopped
1/2 bunch Italian parsley, coarsely
     chopped
     Lemon wedges

TIP   *Serve with hot crusty bread to soak up the delicious sauce.*

Season the scallops with salt and pepper. Heat the olive oil in a shallow skillet until sizzling. Drop the scallops into the hot oil and cook for 1 minute or until a sticky golden crust forms on the underside; do not turn. Turn and cook until golden brown on the remaining side. This process should take 2 to 3 minutes. Remove the scallops to 2 heated plates using a slotted spoon and reserving the pan juices.

Stir the butter into the reserved pan juices; it should melt immediately. Cook until the mixture starts to foam and add the garlic. Swirl the garlic around the pan and add the parsley. Cook until frothy and drizzle over the scallops. Serve immediately with lemon wedges.

Serves 2

sea scallops with saffron couscous

Special enough for company, easy enough for everyday.

1	pound sea scallops, muscles removed
1	teaspoon coarse salt
1/4	teaspoon freshly ground pepper
3	tablespoons olive oil
1/4	cup dry sherry
2 1/2	cups chicken stock
3	tablespoons unsalted butter, cut into pieces
1	tablespoon chopped fresh thyme
1/2	teaspoon salt
1/16	teaspoon saffron
2	cups couscous

Sprinkle the scallops with 1 teaspoon salt and the pepper. Heat 2 tablespoons of the olive oil in a sauté pan over medium-high heat. Cook the scallops in batches in the hot oil for 1 minute per side or until brown and caramelized, adding the remaining 1 tablespoon olive oil if needed. Remove the scallops to a platter using a slotted spoon. Cover to keep warm.

Drain the pan and deglaze with the sherry, stirring with a wooden spoon to dislodge any browned bits. Simmer until the sherry is reduced by 2/3. Add the stock, butter, thyme, 1/2 teaspoon salt and saffron and mix well. Bring to a boil and stir in the couscous. Remove from the heat and cover. Let stand for 5 minutes and fluff with a fork. Serve with the scallops.

Serves 4

shrimp mezcal

We confess—these are our favorite. What's not to like?

1	pound shrimp, peeled and deveined
1/4	cup (1/2 stick) butter
1	ounce mezcal or tequila
1	teaspoon minced garlic
1	avocado, chopped
	Juice of 1 lime
1	teaspoon green jalapeño Tabasco sauce
2	tomatoes, chopped
1/4	cup chopped fresh cilantro

Sauté the shrimp in the butter in a skillet for 1 minute. Add the mezcal and garlic and ignite with a match. As the flame burns down, stir in the avocado, lime juice and jalapeño Tabasco sauce.

Simmer for 3 minutes or until the shrimp turn pink, stirring occasionally. Spoon the shrimp mixture into a bowl and top with the tomatoes and cilantro. Great over rice pilaf or hot cooked pasta.

Serves 2

shrimp mezcal

barbecued shrimp with rémoulade sauce

Much less work than it looks like. Just get moving, and the results will reward you.

RÉMOULADE SAUCE

2	tablespoons finely chopped green onions
1/2	teaspoon finely minced garlic
1/2	cup mayonnaise
1/4	cup finely chopped celery
2	tablespoons finely chopped fresh parsley
2	tablespoons mustard
2	tablespoons horseradish
2	tablespoons ketchup
2	teaspoons lemon juice
2	teaspoons white wine vinegar
1	teaspoon Worcestershire sauce
1/4	teaspoon Tabasco sauce
1/2	teaspoon salt
1/4	teaspoon dry mustard
1/4	teaspoon paprika

BARBECUED SHRIMP

2	tablespoons extra-virgin olive oil
1	tablespoon mild chili powder
1	teaspoon each cumin and salt
1/2	teaspoon sugar
1/2	teaspoon dry mustard
1/2	teaspoon thyme
1/2	teaspoon freshly ground black pepper
1/2	teaspoon curry powder
1/4	teaspoon cayenne pepper
2 1/2	pounds large shrimp (20 per pound), peeled and deveined

SAUCE   Mash the green onions and garlic in a bowl. Stir in the mayonnaise, celery, parsley, prepared mustard, prepared horseradish, ketchup, lemon juice, vinegar, Worcestershire sauce, Tabasco sauce, salt, dry mustard and paprika. Chill, covered with plastic wrap, for 1 to 24 hours. The flavor is best after 24 hours. You may store in the refrigerator for up to 2 weeks.

SHRIMP   Mix 2 tablespoons olive oil, the chili powder, cumin, salt, sugar, dry mustard, thyme, black pepper, curry powder and cayenne pepper in a bowl. Add the shrimp and toss to coat. Marinate, covered, in the refrigerator for 30 minutes.

Preheat the grill or a heavy skillet. Brush the grill rack with additional olive oil and arrange the shrimp on the rack. Grill over hot coals for 1 to 2 minutes per side or just until barely opaque in the center. Arrange on a heated platter and serve with the sauce. You may serve chilled.

Serves 8

Paella is one of the most traditional Spanish dishes out there. It comes from the region of Valencia and takes its name from the special wide, shallow pan it is cooked in. In fact, the correct name for this delicious dinner is Arroz à la Paella, or Rice in the Paella.

classic spanish paella

Really, really worth the work. The ultimate one-pot meal.

2	teaspoons saffron powder
4	cups chicken stock, heated
1/4	cup extra-virgin olive oil
2	garlic cloves
2	cups rice
1	cup peas
2	red bell peppers, sliced
6	artichoke hearts
8	thin slices chorizo or firm sausage
2	cups chopped cooked chicken
8	shrimp, peeled and deveined
16	clams or mussels in shells, scrubbed

Preheat the oven to 350 degrees. Dissolve the saffron powder in the hot stock in a heatproof bowl. Heat the olive oil and garlic in a Dutch oven until heated through and discard the garlic. Stir the rice into the hot garlic oil.

Cook over medium heat until the rice is light brown, stirring frequently. Add the stock mixture and mix well. Stir in the peas, bell peppers, artichokes and chorizo. Adjust the seasonings if desired. Add the chicken, arranging toward the top of the mixture.

Bake, covered, for 1 hour. Remove from the oven and arrange the shrimp and clams in an attractive pattern over the top of the paella. Bake, covered, for 10 to 12 minutes longer or until the clams open.

Serves 6

amaretto chicken with saffron rice

Rich and intense flavors make this a hit for the discerning palate every time.

SAFFRON RICE

1/4	teaspoon saffron
1	tablespoon boiling water
2 1/2	cups chicken broth
1	cup long grain rice
3	tablespoons raisins
1	bay leaf
1	garlic clove, minced
1/2	teaspoon salt
1/8	teaspoon pepper

CHICKEN

4	boneless skinless chicken breasts
2	teaspoons curry powder
1	teaspoon salt
1/4	teaspoon pepper
1/4	cup flour
2	tablespoons butter
16	mushrooms, sliced
1	garlic clove, chopped
3	tablespoons almond liqueur
2	tablespoons lime juice
1	cup chicken broth

RICE   Dissolve the saffron in the boiling water in a saucepan. Add the broth, rice, raisins, bay leaf, garlic, salt and pepper to the saffron mixture and mix well. Cover and bring to a boil; reduce the heat. Simmer, covered, until the rice is tender. Discard the bay leaf.

CHICKEN   Sprinkle the chicken with the curry powder, salt and pepper. Coat the chicken with some of the flour, reserving the remaining flour. Heat the butter in a skillet over medium-high heat. Cook the chicken in the butter until brown on both sides. Stir in the mushrooms, garlic, liqueur and lime juice. Cook for 1 minute, stirring frequently.

Mix the reserved flour with the broth in a small bowl until blended and add to the chicken mixture; reduce the heat to low. Simmer, covered, for 10 to 15 minutes or until the chicken is cooked through, stirring occasionally. Serve with the rice.

Serves 4

sautéed chicken breasts with artichokes and olives

Old world meets new world in this delicious combination of flavors.

4 boneless skinless
chicken breasts
1/16 teaspoon salt
1/16 teaspoon pepper
2 tablespoons olive oil
1 (10-ounce) package frozen
artichokes, thawed and drained
2 tablespoons chopped shallots
1/4 cup dry white wine or
chicken broth
1 tablespoon chopped fresh
rosemary, or 1 teaspoon dried
rosemary
3/4 cup pitted kalamta olives

Pat the chicken dry with paper towels and sprinkle with the salt and pepper. Heat a skillet over medium heat until hot and add the olive oil. Heat until the oil is hot. Add the chicken to the hot oil and cook for 6 to 8 minutes or until brown on both sides, turning only once. Add the artichokes and shallots and mix well. Reduce the heat to low and stir in the wine. Sprinkle with the rosemary.

Cook, covered, for 4 to 5 minutes or until the chicken is cooked through, turning occasionally. Remove the chicken to a platter using a slotted spoon; cover to keep warm. Increase the heat to high and bring the pan juices and artichokes to a boil. Stir in the olives and cook for 1 to 2 minutes or until the liquid is slightly reduced, stirring occasionally. Spoon the sauce and artichokes over the chicken. Serve with hot cooked rice or buttered fettuccini. You may substitute rinsed canned artichokes for the frozen artichokes.

Serves 4

szechuan chicken with peanuts

Sizzle, sizzle. . .hot it may be, but it's irresistible too.

3   tablespoons hoisin sauce
2   tablespoons cornstarch
1   pound boneless skinless chicken
    breasts, cut into strips
1/2 cup chicken broth
2   tablespoons rice vinegar
2   tablespoons sugar
2   teaspoons chili-garlic sauce
1   tablespoon canola oil
1   tablespoon minced fresh
    gingerroot
2   garlic cloves, minced
1   green bell pepper, chopped
2   carrots, diagonally cut into
    thin slices
8   ounces fresh mushrooms, sliced
1/2 cup unsalted dry-roasted
    peanuts

TIP   *Serve with small bowls of
water chestnuts, chopped peanuts,
and green onions to add crunch
and flavor.*

Combine 1 tablespoon of the hoisin sauce and 1 tablespoon of the cornstarch in a bowl and mix well. Add the chicken and toss to coat. Combine the remaining 2 tablespoons hoisin sauce, remaining 1 tablespoon cornstarch, broth, vinegar, sugar and chili-garlic sauce in a bowl and mix well.

Heat a nonstick wok or large deep skillet over medium-high heat until a drop of water sizzles. Add the canola oil to the hot wok and swirl to coat the surface. Stir-fry the chicken in the hot oil for 2 to 3 minutes or until almost cooked through. Add the gingerroot and garlic and stir-fry for 15 seconds or until fragrant. Add the bell pepper, carrots, mushrooms and peanuts.

Stir-fry for 2 minutes or until the vegetables are tender-crisp. Add the hoisin sauce mixture and mix well. Cook for 1 minute or until the chicken is cooked through and the sauce is thickened and bubbly, stirring constantly. Serve immediately.

Serves 4

grilled flank steak with rosemary

Ideal for groups or a quiet dinner for two. . .anytime at all.

1/2 cup soy sauce

1/2 cup olive oil

4 1/2 tablespoons honey

6 garlic cloves, minced

3 tablespoons chopped fresh rosemary

1 1/2 tablespoons coarsely ground pepper

1 1/2 teaspoons salt

2 1/4 pounds flank steak

TIP *Flank steak is the perfect choice for large groups. It is reasonably priced and holds its flavor very well.*

Mix the soy sauce, olive oil, honey, garlic, rosemary, pepper and salt in a 9×13-inch dish. Add the steak and turn to coat. Marinate, covered, in the refrigerator for 2 to 10 hours, turning occasionally; drain.

Preheat the grill. Grill the steak over hot coals for 4 minutes per side for medium-rare or to the desired degree of doneness. Remove the steak to a hard surface and let stand for 5 minutes. Cut the steak across the grain into thin strips. Serve with mashed or roasted potatoes or steamed rice.

Serves 6

saté

A real showstopper with chic Eastern appeal. We love it!

BEEF
1 1/2 pounds lean beef sirloin or beef
  round steak
2 tablespoons soy sauce
1 tablespoon cumin
1 tablespoon coriander
1 garlic clove, minced or crushed
1 tablespoon vegetable oil

MARINATED CUCUMBERS
2 large cucumbers
1 cup vinegar
1/2 cup sugar

BASTING SAUCE
3 tablespoons fresh lemon juice
2 tablespoons soy sauce
1/2 teaspoon curry
1/4 teaspoon cumin
1/4 teaspoon coriander

PEANUT SAUCE AND ASSEMBLY
1 cup water
1 cup peanut butter
2 garlic cloves, minced
1 small onion, minced
1/4 cup chopped seeded hot
  red chiles
2 tablespoons brown sugar
2 tablespoons fresh lemon juice
2 tablespoons soy sauce

BEEF   Cut the beef into 1/2-inch cubes or strips. Combine the soy sauce, cumin, coriander, garlic and oil in a shallow dish and mix well. Add the beef and turn to coat. Marinate, covered, in the refrigerator for 8 to 10 hours, turning occasionally. You may substitute pork rump or leg or chicken breasts for the beef.

CUCUMBERS   Thinly slice the cucumbers. Combine the vinegar and sugar in a bowl and stir until the sugar dissolves. Add the cucumbers and stir until coated. Chill for 2 hours.

BASTING SAUCE   Combine the lemon juice, soy sauce, curry, cumin and coriander in a bowl and mix well. Chill.

PEANUT SAUCE   Combine the water, peanut butter and garlic in a small saucepan and mix well. Cook over medium-low heat until the mixture boils and thickens, stirring constantly. Remove from the heat and stir in the red chiles, brown sugar, lemon juice and soy sauce. Chill, covered, in the refrigerator.

ASSEMBLY   Soak bamboo skewers in water for 15 minutes; drain. Preheat the grill to medium. Thread about 4 beef cubes or beef strips per skewer and arrange on a lightly greased grill rack 4 to 6 inches from the heat source. Grill for 8 to 10 minutes for medium-rare, turning and basting frequently with the Basting Sauce. Grill pork for about 15 minutes and chicken for about 8 minutes. You may broil if desired. Reheat the Peanut Sauce in a saucepan over low heat, adding additional water as needed for a medium-thick sauce, and pour into a small heatproof bowl. Arrange the sauce and cucumbers on a serving tray and surround with the skewers.

Serves 4 to 6

grilled beef salad with caramelized onions

A salad men will line up for.

BLUE CHEESE DRESSING

3   ounces blue cheese, crumbled
2   tablespoons hot water
1/3 cup mayonnaise
1/3 cup sour cream
    Freshly ground black pepper
    to taste

SALAD

2   tablespoons olive oil
8   slices sourdough bread, cubed
1/2 cup (2 ounces) freshly grated
    Parmesan cheese
3   tablespoons Worcestershire
    sauce
2   tablespoons olive oil
1   pound beef tenderloin, trimmed
    and cut into 1/2-inch-thick slices
2   garlic cloves, thinly sliced
2 1/2 pounds onions, cut into
    1/4-inch-thick slices
2   tablespoons olive oil
2   tablespoons balsamic vinegar
    Salt and freshly ground pepper
    to taste
2   tablespoons olive oil
10 ounces shiitake mushrooms or
    chanterelles
    Olive oil to taste
10 ounces escarole or any type
    of lettuce

DRESSING   Combine the blue cheese and hot water in a bowl and stir until smooth. Stir in the mayonnaise, sour cream and pepper. Chill, covered, for up to 3 days.

SALAD   Heat 2 tablespoons olive oil in a 12-inch skillet. Add the bread cubes and sprinkle with the cheese. Cook until brown and crisp on all sides, turning frequently. Drizzle the Worcestershire sauce and 2 tablespoons olive oil over the beef in a nonreactive dish and toss to coat. Sprinkle with the garlic. Marinate, covered, in the refrigerator for 1 hour or longer, turning occasionally. Bring to room temperature before cooking.

Preheat the oven to 375 degrees. Cut the onion slices into halves. Coat a baking sheet with a mixture of 2 tablespoons olive oil and the vinegar. Arrange the onions on the prepared baking sheet and sprinkle with salt and pepper. Bake for 20 minutes or until caramelized on the bottom; turn the onions. Drizzle with additional oil and vinegar if needed. Bake for 10 to 15 minutes longer or until caramelized on the remaining side.

Heat 2 tablespoons olive oil in a large skillet until very hot. Add the mushrooms and sprinkle with salt and pepper. Cook until the moisture evaporates and the mushrooms are light brown, stirring frequently. Heat enough olive oil to cover the bottom of a large skillet over medium-high heat. Add half the beef and sprinkle with salt and pepper. Sear for 1 to 2 minutes or until brown, turning once. Remove to a platter and repeat with the remaining beef. Toss the escarole and dressing in a bowl and portion evenly on 4 serving plates. Sprinkle with the onions and mushrooms. Arrange the beef over the top of each salad and sprinkle with the croutons. Serve with any remaining dressing.

Serves 4

grilled pork tenderloin with tortillas and guacamole

A great, really original way to serve pork. Definitely NOT your grandmother's pork chops.

GUACAMOLE

2	or 3 large ripe avocados
1	large ripe tomato, seeded and chopped
1	garlic clove, minced
2	tablespoons chopped fresh cilantro
2	tablespoons (or more) fresh lime juice
1/4	teaspoon (more or less) Tabasco sauce
1	teaspoon minced fresh jalapeño chile (optional)
	Salt and pepper to taste

PORK

2	(1-pound) pork tenderloins, trimmed
1/2	cup dry red or white wine
2	tablespoons balsamic vinegar or red wine vinegar
2	tablespoons olive oil
2	teaspoons chopped fresh thyme, or 1/2 teaspoon dried thyme
1/2	teaspoon salt
1/4	teaspoon freshly ground pepper
	Vegetable oil
	Warm tortillas

GUACAMOLE Coarsely mash the avocados in a bowl, leaving a few small lumps. Stir in the tomato, garlic and cilantro. Add the lime juice, Tabasco sauce and jalapeño chile and mix gently. Season with salt and pepper. Press a sheet of plastic wrap directly onto the surface of the guacamole and chill until serving time.

PORK Arrange the tenderloins in a shallow nonreactive dish. Whisk the wine, vinegar, olive oil, thyme, salt and pepper in a bowl and pour over the tenderloins, turning to coat. Marinate, covered, in the refrigerator for 2 hours or longer, turning occasionally.

Preheat the grill and place the grill rack 4 to 6 inches above the coals. Lightly brush the rack with vegetable oil. Drain the tenderloins and pat dry with paper towels, reserving the marinade. Arrange on the prepared grill rack.

Grill the tenderloins for 25 minutes or until a meat thermometer registers 160 degrees for medium, turning frequently and basting with the reserved marinade occasionally. Let stand for 5 minutes before carving. Cut the tenderloins diagonally into thin slices and serve with the Guacamole and tortillas.

Serves 4 to 6

pork medallions with port and cranberry sauce

The perfect cold-weather warmer. A family favorite that's fit for company.

1/2 cup dried cranberries, dried cherries or dried pitted prunes
1 cup water
1 teaspoon vegetable oil
1 (1-pound) pork tenderloin, trimmed and cut into 12 medallions
   Salt and freshly ground pepper to taste
1 shallot, minced
1/2 cup port
1/4 cup balsamic vinegar
1 cup skimmed reduced-sodium chicken stock
1/2 teaspoon thyme
1 teaspoon cornstarch
1 tablespoon water

Combine the cranberries and 1 cup water in a saucepan and bring to a simmer. Simmer for 3 minutes, stirring occasionally. Drain, reserving both the cranberries and the cooking liquid.

Heat the oil in a large nonstick skillet over medium heat. Sprinkle the pork with salt and pepper and add to the hot oil. Cook for 3 minutes per side or until brown and no longer pink internally but still juicy. Remove the pork to a platter with a slotted spoon, reserving the pan drippings. Cover loosely to keep warm.

Cook the shallot in the reserved pan drippings for 30 seconds, stirring constantly. Stir in the wine and vinegar. Bring to a boil, stirring with a wooden spoon to dislodge any browned bits. Boil for 3 to 5 minutes or until the mixture is reduced by 1/2, stirring occasionally. Add the stock, thyme and reserved cooking liquid and mix well. Return to a boil and boil for 5 to 7 minutes longer or until the mixture is reduced by 1/2, stirring occasionally.

Dissolve the cornstarch in 1 tablespoon water in a small bowl and whisk into the sauce. Cook until shiny and slightly thickened, stirring constantly. Stir in the reserved cranberries and season with salt and pepper. Simmer just until heated through, stirring frequently. Spoon the sauce over the medallions and serve immediately.

Serves 4

Dessert: we can't think of a downside to this kind of "hit and run" entertaining—except that not enough people are doing it.

dessert

We love having friends over for dessert. Who wouldn't—for the hostess it's quick and easy with a defined timeline; for the guests it's the perfect opportunity to drop in, chat, and hit the road without fear of rudeness. And, of course, there's never any question of what to do with all the leftovers. In fact, we can't think of a downside to this kind of "hit and run" entertaining—except that not enough people are doing it.

Dessert is special on so many levels—it satisfies the basic human desire for sweet, creamy things; it allows the chef to express herself (or himself!) with love and creativity; and it's the perfect showcase for all the wonderful, local fruits that made California famous. For example, we don't know of any better use for the noble strawberry than to put it in a pie, delicately folded into rich, flaky pastry, topped with real French vanilla bean ice cream. Or how about offering someone special a delectable slice of Chocolate Macadamia Torte, rich and utterly satisfying with every bite?

Truly, dessert is the perfect punctuation mark to an evening spent with friends. And as for your family? Well, we know there won't be any sullen faces when our unbelievable Chocolate Chocolate Chip Cheesecake hits the table— what a fabulous way (and a remarkably easy one, all things considered) to say "Well done," or "Congratulations," or even "We all love you."

Making dessert is a great bonding ritual, too—children don't seem to see it as "work," especially when there's a bowl or beater to lick. Having problems communicating with your teenager? Spend an afternoon peeling fruit and rolling pastry together for our California Pear Pie, and you'll be surprised at how easy it is to talk, hands busy in the kitchen. And isn't that reward alone worth blowing the diet for—at least a little bit?

california pear pie

Not just for the holidays, this pie gets rave reviews any time of the year.

2	refrigerator pie pastries
2	(29-ounce) cans pears, drained and chopped
3/4	cup sugar
3/4	cup half-and-half
1 1/2	tablespoons fresh orange juice
1 1/2	tablespoons fresh lemon juice
1/16	teaspoon salt
1 1/2	tablespoons cornstarch
1	tablespoon butter
1/4	teaspoon cinnamon
1/4	teaspoon nutmeg

TIP *Have fun with the top pie pastry. Try cutting out hearts for Valentine's Day or a flag design for the Fourth of July. The sky's the limit.*

Preheat the oven to 425 degrees. Fit 1 of the pastries into a pie plate and mound the pears in the prepared pie plate. Mix the sugar, half-and-half, orange juice, lemon juice and salt in a bowl. Whisk the cornstarch into the half-and-half mixture until blended and pour over the pears. Dot with the butter and sprinkle with the cinnamon and nutmeg. Top with the remaining pastry, fluting the edge and cutting vents.

Bake for 15 minutes. Reduce the heat to 350 degrees and bake for 45 minutes longer. Serve warm or chilled with ice cream. You may substitute 1/2 teaspoon pumpkin spice for the 1/4 teaspoon cinnamon and 1/4 teaspoon nutmeg. Substitute 5 chopped peeled fresh pears for the canned pears if desired.

Serves 6

bourbon pecan pie

Rich, rich, rich—and good, good, good.

PASTRY

1 1/2 cups flour

2 tablespoons plus 1 teaspoon brown sugar

1/2 teaspoon vanilla extract

1/2 teaspoon white vinegar

1/8 teaspoon salt

1/2 cup (1 stick) plus 3 tablespoons butter, melted

PECAN FILLING

6 eggs

1/4 cup packed brown sugar

1/4 cup sugar

1 teaspoon flour

3/4 teaspoon baking soda

1/8 teaspoon salt

1 1/2 cups dark corn syrup

1/4 cup bourbon

1 teaspoon vanilla extract

3/4 cup pecan pieces

1/4 cup semisweet chocolate chips

TIP   *Serve with a dollop of barely sweetened whipped cream and a hot cup of coffee. This is casual dessert dining at its best.*

PASTRY   Combine the flour, brown sugar, vanilla, vinegar and salt in a bowl and mix well. Add the butter gradually, stirring constantly until the mixture forms a dough. Pat the dough over the bottom and up the side of a 10-inch pie plate sprayed with nonstick cooking spray.

FILLING   Preheat the oven to 300 degrees. Beat the eggs in a mixing bowl until blended. Mix the brown sugar, sugar, flour, baking soda and salt in a bowl and add to the eggs. Beat until blended. Add the corn syrup, bourbon and vanilla and beat until smooth. Stir in the pecans and chocolate chips.

Spoon the pecan mixture into the pastry-lined pie plate. Bake for 45 to 50 minutes or until the crust is brown and the filling is set. Let stand until cool.

Serves 8 to 10

mocha pie

This is one special pie, and worth the effort. Just don't tell your dieting friends what they are eating.

CHOCOLATE CRUST

18	chocolate wafer cookies
1/3	cup butter, melted

CHOCOLATE SAUCE

2	ounces unsweetened chocolate
1/2	cup sugar
1	tablespoon butter
1	(5-ounce) can evaporated milk

PIE

1	quart coffee ice cream, slightly thawed
1	cup whipping cream
2	tablespoons (or more) Kahlúa
	Sugar to taste
1/2	cup chopped nuts

CRUST   Finely crush the cookies. Combine the cookie crumbs and butter in a bowl and mix well. Press the crumb mixture over the bottom and up the side of a 10-inch pie plate. Chill in the refrigerator.

SAUCE   Heat the chocolate in a double boiler over hot water until melted, stirring occasionally. Stir in the sugar and butter. Add the evaporated milk gradually, stirring constantly. Cook over hot water until thickened and of a sauce consistency, stirring frequently. Chill, covered, for 45 minutes.

PIE   Spread the ice cream in the prepared pie plate and freeze for 1 hour or until firm. Spread with the sauce. Beat the whipping cream in a mixing bowl until soft peaks form. Add the liqueur and sugar and mix well. Spread over the prepared layers, sealing to the edge. Sprinkle with the nuts and freeze until firm. Let stand at room temperature for several minutes before serving.

Serves 8 to 10

strawberry pie

This will make your home smell like summer.

CRUST

50	vanilla wafers
1/4	cup (1/2 stick) butter or margarine, melted
2	tablespoons sugar
1	teaspoon grated orange zest

STRAWBERRY FILLING

2	cups ripe strawberries, hulled
1/2	cup water
1/2	cup sugar
2	tablespoons cornstarch
3/4	teaspoon lemon juice
6	cups small ripe strawberries, hulled
1/2	cup whipped cream

TIP *When buying flats of strawberries, remember not to rinse the berries until just before you plan to use them. Once rinsed, strawberries spoil very quickly, but they will last, unrinsed and chilled, for up to one week.*

CRUST Preheat the oven to 350 degrees. Process the wafers in a food processor until finely ground. Add the butter, sugar and orange zest and pulse just until combined. Pat the crumb mixture over the bottom and up the side of a greased 9-inch pie plate. Bake for 15 minutes. Cool on a wire rack.

FILLING Mash 2 cups strawberries in a saucepan using a potato masher. Stir in the water. Bring to a boil and cook for 5 minutes, stirring occasionally. Press the strawberry mixture through a sieve into a bowl, discarding the solids and reserving 1 cup of the liquid. Add additional water if needed to measure 1 cup.

Combine the sugar and cornstarch in a saucepan and mix well. Stir in the reserved liquid. Bring to a boil and boil for 1 minute, stirring constantly. Reduce the heat and cook for 2 minutes, stirring frequently. Stir in the lemon juice.

Arrange just enough of the 6 cups strawberries to form 1 layer over the baked crust. Spoon about 1/3 of the sauce over the strawberries and top with the remaining strawberries and remaining sauce. Chill for 3 hours or longer. Serve with the whipped cream.

Serves 8

chocolate chocolate chip cheesecake

Chocolate and cheesecake lovers unite!

CHOCOLATE COOKIE CRUST

3¹/2 tablespoons butter
1 cup finely crushed chocolate wafer cookies
2 tablespoons sugar

CHEESECAKE

2 pounds cream cheese, softened
1 cup sugar
4 eggs
1¹/2 cups sour cream
2 teaspoons vanilla extract
1 cup (6 ounces) miniature semisweet chocolate chips
8 ounces semisweet chocolate, melted

TIP *To make this cake even more elegant for special occasions, serve garnished with fresh raspberries and dark chocolate curls. For chocolate curls, microwave a bar of semisweet chocolate on Defrost just until slightly softened. Use a vegetable peeler to form the curls.*

CRUST Heat the butter in a saucepan until melted. Remove from the heat and stir in the wafer crumbs and sugar. Pat the crumb mixture over the bottom of an oiled 9-inch springform pan. Freeze in the freezer.

CHEESECAKE Preheat the oven to 275 degrees. Beat the cream cheese and sugar in a mixing bowl until creamy. Add the eggs 2 at a time, beating well after each addition. Stir in the sour cream and vanilla. Fold in the chocolate chips and melted chocolate.

Spread the cream cheese mixture over the frozen crust and tap the pan on the countertop to break any large air bubbles. Wrap the bottom and side of the pan with heavy-duty foil.

Place the springform pan in a larger baking pan and fill the baking pan with enough water to measure 2 inches. Bake for 1¹/2 to 2 hours or just until the center is almost set. Remove the foil and place the pan on a wire rack. Cool for 45 minutes. Chill, covered, on the rack for 5 hours or longer.

Serves 12 to 16

pumpkin cheesecake

Perfect for fall and a flavorful variation on traditional cheesecake.

CRUST

1¹/4 cups fine gingersnap cookie crumbs

¹/4 cup (¹/2 stick) butter, melted

PUMPKIN FILLING

24 ounces cream cheese, softened

1 cup sugar

1 teaspoon cinnamon

1 teaspoon ginger

¹/2 teaspoon ground cloves

1 (16-ounce) can pumpkin

4 eggs

³/4 cup whipping cream, chilled

TIP   *Add some extra snap by using crushed Hot and Spicy Gingersnaps (page 108) for the crust.*

CRUST   Preheat the oven to 350 degrees. Mix the cookie crumbs and butter in a bowl and pat the crumb mixture over the bottom of a 9-inch springform pan. Bake for 10 minutes. Cool on a wire rack. Reduce the oven temperature to 300 degrees.

FILLING   Combine the cream cheese, sugar, cinnamon, ginger and cloves in a mixing bowl and beat at medium speed until smooth and fluffy, scraping the bowl occasionally. Add the pumpkin to the cream cheese mixture and beat until smooth. Add the eggs 1 at a time, beating at low speed just until blended after each addition. Spread the pumpkin mixture over the baked layer.

Bake for 1 hour or until the cheesecake tests done. Cool on a wire rack for 20 minutes. Chill, covered, for 3 hours but no longer than 48 hours. Run a sharp knife around the edge of the cheesecake and remove the side. Beat the whipping cream in a chilled bowl until soft peaks form. Top each serving with a dollop of whipped cream.

Serves 12

brownie pudding

A League family favorite that we know you will love too.

2   teaspoons butter
1   cup flour
3/4 cup sugar
2   tablespoons (rounded) baking
     cocoa
2   teaspoons baking powder
1/2 teaspoon salt
1/2 cup milk
1   teaspoon vanilla extract
1 1/2 cups boiling water
1   cup sugar
1/4 cup baking cocoa

Preheat the oven to 350 degrees. Heat the butter in a 7×9-inch baking pan or 9-inch round baking dish until melted and tilt the pan to ensure even coverage. Let stand until cool. Combine the flour, 3/4 cup sugar, 2 tablespoons baking cocoa, baking powder and salt in a heatproof bowl and mix well. Stir in the milk and vanilla and spoon the chocolate batter into the prepared pan; the batter will be stiff.

Mix the boiling water, 1 cup sugar and 1/4 cup baking cocoa in the same bowl and pour over the prepared layer. Bake for 45 minutes. Serve warm with ice cream.

Serves 4 to 6

These cakes should be slightly underbaked, in order to get a true "molten" chocolate center. For even more luxury, drizzle caramel sauce on the dessert plate before serving, and add a side of French vanilla bean ice cream.

molten chocolate cakes

Surprisingly simple!

5	ounces bittersweet or semisweet chocolate, chopped
10	tablespoons (1 1/4 sticks) unsalted butter
3	eggs
3	egg yolks
1 1/2	cups confectioners' sugar
1/2	cup flour

TIP   *You can make this cake even easier to prepare by substituting chocolate chips and melting the chocolate chips in the microwave. If you are doing it the old-fashioned way, melted chocolate scorches easily and will seize or clump up without warning if it comes in contact with moisture. To avoid this unhappy occurrence, follow these simple guidelines: do not store chocolate in the refrigerator or freezer; make sure all utensils are perfectly dry; and chop or grate the chocolate into uniformly small pieces, which will melt quickly before any section has a chance to scorch. Place the chocolate in a bowl over simmering water or in a microwave and heat until completely smooth.*

Preheat the oven to 450 degrees. Coat six 3/4-cup soufflé dishes or custard cups with butter. Combine the chocolate and butter in a heavy medium saucepan. Cook over low heat until melted, stirring frequently. Cool slightly. Whisk the eggs and egg yolks in a bowl until blended. Whisk the confectioners' sugar into the eggs until smooth. Add the chocolate mixture and whisk until blended. Whisk in the flour.

Spoon the batter evenly into the prepared dishes. You may prepare to this point up to 1 day in advance and store, covered, in the refrigerator. Bake for 11 to 14 minutes or until the sides are set but the center is soft and runny. Run a sharp knife around the edge of the cakes and immediately invert onto dessert plates. Serve immediately, garnished with whipped cream.

Serves 6

This is a basic, intense, chocolate hedonist's cake. It is a quickie to bake and can be enjoyed as is, with a dollop of whipped cream, vanilla gelato, and/or raspberry sauce. For a special occasion, really pull out all the stops and spin caramel ribbons on top. It can be prepared several days in advance. And like many of us, it just gets better with age.

chocolate macadamia torte

When you really mean business, this is the dessert to make.

1	pound bittersweet chocolate
1	cup (2 sticks) unsalted butter, chopped and softened
6	ounces (about $1/4$ cup) unsalted macadamia nuts, well toasted
$1^1/2$	cups sugar
10	egg yolks, at room temperature
$1/4$	cup rum or Grand Marnier
10	egg whites, at room temperature
$1/8$	teaspoon cream of tartar
	Confectioners' sugar to taste

Preheat the oven to 250 degrees. Process the chocolate in a food processor until finely chopped. Combine the chocolate and butter in a double boiler and heat over simmering water until blended, stirring frequently. Let stand until cool. Combine the macadamia nuts and $1/4$ cup of the sugar in a food processor and pulse until finely ground.

Place the egg yolks in a mixing bowl. Add 1 cup of the remaining sugar gradually, beating constantly until thick and pale yellow in color. The egg yolk mixture should form a ribbon when the beaters are lifted. Add the chocolate mixture to the egg yolk mixture and beat at low speed until blended. Add the rum gradually and beat until smooth. Stir in the macadamia nut mixture.

Beat the egg whites and cream of tartar in a mixing bowl until soft peaks form. Add the remaining $1/4$ cup sugar 1 tablespoon at a time to the egg whites, beating constantly until stiff peaks form. Fold $1/4$ of the egg whites into the egg yolk mixture. Fold the egg yolk mixture into the egg whites. Spoon the batter into a buttered and lightly floured 12-inch springform pan.

Bake for $2^3/4$ to 3 hours or until the cake pulls from the side of the pan and a wooden pick inserted in the center comes out clean. Cool in the pan for 10 minutes. Remove to a wire rack to cool completely. The cake will sink in the center as it cools. Store, wrapped in foil, at room temperature or in the refrigerator. If chilled, bring to room temperature before serving. Slice and sprinkle with confectioners' sugar. Serve with whipped cream, raspberry sauce and/or vanilla gelato.

Serves 12

christmas morning cake

Pretty, tangy, tart, and sweet. This is one cake you will want to make all year round.

1/4 cup (1/2 stick) unsalted butter

3/4 cup superfine sugar

2 cups cranberries or berries in season

1 cup self-rising flour

1/2 cup (1 stick) unsalted butter

1 teaspoon cinnamon

1/16 teaspoon salt

2/3 cup superfine sugar

2 eggs

1 1/2 tablespoons milk

Preheat the oven to 350 degrees. Place a baking sheet in the oven at the same time. Heat 1/4 cup butter in a 10-inch baking pan or tarte-Tatin dish over medium heat until melted. Stir in 3/4 cup sugar. Add the cranberries and stir until coated.

Combine the self-rising flour, 1/2 cup butter, cinnamon, salt, 2/3 cup sugar and eggs in a food processor. Pulse while adding enough milk through the funnel until the batter is of a soft consistency. Pour the batter over the cranberry mixture and place the baking pan on the preheated baking sheet.

Bake for 30 minutes or until the cake is brown and puffy and the edges have begun to pull from the side of the pan. Remove from the oven and place a serving plate on top of the pan and invert. Serve warm with ice cream.

Serves 6

pineapple meringue cake

One bite of this, and you will know it was worth the effort.

CAKE

1	cup sifted cake flour
2	teaspoons baking powder
1/8	teaspoon salt
4	egg whites
1	cup sugar
1	teaspoon vanilla extract
1/2	cup shortening
1/2	cup sugar
4	egg yolks
5	tablespoons milk
1	teaspoon vanilla extract
3/4	cup finely chopped pecans

PINEAPPLE CREAM FILLING AND ASSEMBLY

1	cup whipping cream
1 1/2	teaspoons confectioners' sugar
1/4	teaspoon vanilla extract
1	(15-ounce) can crushed pineapple, drained

CAKE   Preheat the oven to 350 degrees. Sift the cake flour, baking powder and salt together. Beat the egg whites in a mixing bowl until soft peaks form. Add 1 cup sugar gradually, beating constantly until stiff peaks form. Fold in 1 teaspoon vanilla.

Beat the shortening and 1/2 cup sugar in a mixing bowl until creamy. Add the egg yolks and beat until blended. Add the cake flour mixture and milk alternately to the creamed mixture, mixing well after each addition. Stir in 1 teaspoon vanilla.

Spoon the batter evenly into 2 greased and floured 8-inch cake pans. Spread each with 1/2 of the meringue and sprinkle equally with the pecans. Bake for 40 to 45 minutes or until the cake tests done and the meringue is light brown. Cool in the pans on a wire rack. Run a sharp knife around the edges of the layers and remove to a wire rack. The meringue will often spread or be a little crumbly in texture. Do not panic. Just press together with hands to shape if necessary.

FILLING   Beat the whipping cream in a mixing bowl until soft peaks form. Add the confectioners' sugar and vanilla and mix well. Fold in the pineapple.

ASSEMBLY   Arrange 1 cake layer meringue side down on a cake plate and spread with the filling. Top with the remaining cake layer meringue side up. Chill, covered with plastic wrap, for 2 to 10 hours. The cake and filling will mellow while chilling.

Serves 12

pineapple meringue cake

Every month, JLSD honors its hardest-working volunteers at the general meeting by presenting them with a golden tiara in front of the entire membership. This cake was first served at a board meeting and was named the Golden Tiara Cake in honor of our awards. For a big effect, we serve it in a bundt pan with a golden tiara in the center. We all love this tradition and hope you will want to give it a place in your family too.

golden tiara cake

Known as Sour Cream Pecan Brittle Cake to outsiders. To us, it's part of the JLSD family.

CAKE

1	(2-layer) package yellow cake mix
4	eggs
1	cup sour cream
1/3	cup vegetable oil
1/2	teaspoon vanilla extract
1/2	teaspoon almond extract
2	ounces bittersweet or semisweet chocolate, coarsely grated

PECAN BRITTLE

3/4	cup sugar
1/4	cup water
1/8	teaspoon cream of tartar
3/4	cup pecan halves, toasted and coarsely chopped

BROWN SUGAR FROSTING AND ASSEMBLY

1/2	cup packed dark brown sugar
3	tablespoons water
1/4	cup heavy cream
3	cups (or more) confectioners' sugar
1/2	cup (1 stick) unsalted butter, softened

CAKE   Preheat the oven to 350 degrees. Spray a bundt pan or two 9-inch cake pans with nonstick cooking spray. Combine the cake mix, eggs, sour cream, oil and flavorings in a mixing bowl and beat for 3 minutes or until blended, scraping the bowl occasionally. Fold in the chocolate.

Spoon the batter into the prepared bundt pan. Bake for 30 to 32 minutes or until a wooden pick inserted near the center comes out clean and the top is golden brown. Cool in the pan for 10 minutes and loosen the edge of the cake with a sharp knife. Remove to a wire rack to cool completely. If baking in two 9-inch cake pans, bake for 28 to 32 minutes or until a wooden pick inserted in the center comes out clean and the tops are brown. Cool in the pans for 10 minutes and run a sharp knife around the edges of the layers to loosen. Remove to a wire rack to cool completely.

BRITTLE   Spray a baking sheet with sides with nonstick cooking spray. Combine the sugar, water and cream of tartar in a heavy saucepan and mix well. Cook over medium-low heat until the sugar dissolves, stirring constantly. Increase the heat to high and bring to a boil; do not stir. Boil for 9 to 11 minutes or until the syrup is deep amber in color, occasionally brushing down the side of the pan with a wet pastry brush. Add the pecans and swirl to combine. Pour the pecan mixture onto the prepared baking sheet and spread evenly. Let stand until cool. Break into small pieces or place the brittle in a resealable plastic bag and crush with a meat mallet. You may prepare the brittle up to 1 week in advance and store in an airtight container.

TIP *When the cake is cool enough to handle but still slightly hot to the touch, run a small sharp knife around the edge of the cake to loosen. Cover the cake with waxed paper, top with a rack or large flat plate, and invert. The cake will fall from the pan. Remove the pan and pan lining if necessary, cover with a cooling rack, and invert again. Remove the top rack or plate and paper. When using a bundt pan, use dental floss to slice neat, even pieces.*

FROSTING Combine the brown sugar and water in a heavy saucepan and mix well. Cook over medium-low heat until the sugar dissolves, stirring frequently. Increase the heat and bring to a boil. Boil for 3 minutes or until slightly thickened, stirring frequently. Do not overcook, as the frosting will become too thick to use. Remove from the heat and cool for 5 minutes. Stir in the heavy cream.

Beat 3 cups confectioners' sugar and the butter in a mixing bowl until creamy. Add the brown sugar mixture and beat until blended. Add enough additional confectioners' sugar until the frosting is of a spreading consistency and mix well.

ASSEMBLY Cut the bundt cake horizontally into halves using dental floss or fishing line. Arrange the bottom half cut side up on a cake platter. Spread with 1 cup of the frosting and sprinkle with 1/2 cup of the brittle, pressing lightly. Top with the remaining cake layer cut side down. Spread the remaining frosting over the top and side of the cake and sprinkle with the remaining brittle. You may prepare up to 1 day in advance and store, covered, in the refrigerator. Let stand at room temperature for 1 hour before serving.

Serves 16

margarita cake

This deceptively simple cake snuck into our hearts and just won't leave.

CAKE

1³/4	cups sugar
1/2	cup (1 stick) butter, softened
1/2	teaspoon baking soda
1/4	teaspoon salt
3	eggs
1	tablespoon grated lemon zest
1	tablespoon fresh lemon juice
2¹/2	cups flour
1	cup lemon or plain yogurt

LIME GLAZE AND ASSEMBLY

1/2	cup sugar
2	tablespoons fresh lime juice (preferably Mexican limes)
1	tablespoon water
1	tablespoon tequila

CAKE   Preheat the oven to 350 degrees. Combine the sugar, butter, baking soda and salt in a mixing bowl and beat until blended. Add the eggs 1 at a time, beating well and scraping the bowl after each addition. Mix in the lemon zest and lemon juice. Add the flour and yogurt alternately, beating well after each addition.

Spoon the batter into a greased and floured 9×13-inch cake pan. Bake for 25 to 30 minutes or until a wooden pick inserted in the center comes out clean. Cool in the pan on a wire rack for 15 minutes.

GLAZE   Combine the sugar, lime juice and water in a saucepan and mix well. Cook until the sugar dissolves, stirring frequently. Stir in the tequila.

ASSEMBLY   Invert the warm cake onto a serving platter and brush with the glaze until it is absorbed. Let stand until cool. Slice and garnish each serving with a lime slice and a dollop of whipped cream.

Serves 16

margarita cake

strawberry shortcake

Forget your preconceptions of strawberry shortcake. This is rich, elegant, and delicious.

BRANDY SAUCE

8	egg yolks, lightly beaten
1/4	cup sugar
1/4	cup framboise or kirsch
1 1/4	cups whipping cream

STRAWBERRY FILLING

4	pints fresh strawberries, thickly sliced
1/4 to 1/2	cup confectioners' sugar, or to taste
1	tablespoon framboise or kirsch

SHORTCAKE AND ASSEMBLY

2	cups flour
1	tablespoon baking powder
1/2	teaspoon salt
2	tablespoons sugar
6	tablespoons unsalted butter, cut into 1/2-inch pieces and chilled
1	cup heavy cream

SAUCE   Combine the egg yolks, sugar and brandy in a double boiler and mix well. Cook over simmering water until the mixture becomes foamy and begins to thicken, whisking constantly. Remove from the heat. Whisk in 1/4 cup of the whipping cream. Pour the sauce into a bowl and let stand until cool. Beat the remaining 1 cup of whipping cream in a mixing bowl until stiff peaks form. Fold the whipped cream into the cooled sauce. Chill, covered, up to 1 day in advance.

FILLING   Process 2 cups of the strawberries in a food processor until puréed. Combine the purée, remaining strawberries, confectioners' sugar and brandy in a bowl and mix gently. You may prepare up to 8 hours in advance and chill.

SHORTCAKE   Preheat the oven to 425 degrees. Combine the flour, baking powder, salt and sugar in a food processor and process just until mixed. Add the butter and pulse until the consistency of bread crumbs. Add the heavy cream gradually, processing constantly until the mixture forms a soft dough.

Knead the dough on a lightly floured surface. Roll 1/2 inch thick and cut into 3-inch rounds. Arrange the rounds 2 inches apart on an ungreased baking sheet. Bake for 10 to 12 minutes or until light brown. Remove to a wire rack to cool. The shortcakes are best if baked no more than 2 hours before serving.

ASSEMBLY   Split the shortcakes horizontally into halves and arrange 2 halves cut side up on dessert plates. Spoon 2 tablespoons of the filling on each half and drizzle with 2 tablespoons of the sauce. Serve with the remaining sauce.

Serves 8

the best sugar cookies

Look no further for the perfect sugar cookie.

4 cups flour
1 cup sugar
1 cup confectioners' sugar
1 cup (2 sticks) unsalted butter, softened
3/4 cup vegetable oil
1 teaspoon baking soda
1 teaspoon cream of tartar
1 teaspoon salt
1 teaspoon vanilla extract
Sugar to taste

Preheat the oven to 350 degrees. Combine the flour, 1 cup sugar, confectioners' sugar, butter, oil, baking soda, cream of tartar, salt and vanilla in a mixing bowl in the order listed, mixing well after each addition. Shape the dough into 1-inch balls and coat with additional granulated sugar.

Arrange the balls 2 inches apart on a baking sheet and flatten slightly with a glass dipped in sugar. Bake for 15 minutes or until light brown. Cool on the cookie sheet for 2 minutes. Remove to a wire rack to cool completely. Store in an airtight container.

Makes 5 dozen cookies

It's easy to see why
we find it hard to stop
the party once we
get home.

midnight snack

Here in San Diego, we are lucky enough to have great nightlife spots available to us all year round. (This is handy, because we also get visitors all year round!) In the summer, we can treat ourselves to an evening out at the Starlight Theater to catch a musical in the moonlight; or it's a fun expedition with the kids to check out the Nighttime Zoo and watch the fireworks rise over Sea World on the way home. As the holiday season gets into full swing, the Parade of Lights on Mission Bay is a must-go tradition, as the yachts float by in full lighted beauty. The historic Gaslamp District is always fun, of course, but during the winter, when the locals threaten to outnumber the tourists, it's an especially lively experience; and we know spring has sprung when the hard-core beach dwellers start firing up their seaside barbecue pits.

With all that going on, it's easy to see why we find it hard to stop the party once we get home, and why we love to have a battery of so-easy, never-fail, no-effort recipes at hand. These secret weapons have saved us more than once, and while some of them may be pretty simple, the results are simply pretty. If you won't tell how easy our Clam Toasties are to make, we won't—and we won't breathe a word when you claim our Banker's Hill Beer as an old family recipe.

Whether you've spent the day working hard, or hardly working, it's always fun to entertain good friends in a casual setting, and that's what the midnight snack is all about. We know you may not thank us for keeping the party spirit alive tonight when the alarm goes off tomorrow morning, but hey—life is short. Why don't you worry about that mañana?

Founded in the 1850s, Banker's Hill is one of San Diego's oldest neighborhoods. It's loaded with character and features fabulous Victorian architecture, with mansions overlooking the Bay. In fact, until the I-5 was completed, this area had some of the most unobstructed views in San Diego. At the heart of Banker's Hill is Balboa Park, the Central Park of San Diego. It's close to our hearts, too—our house is located right in the middle of this historic district, at 210 Maple Street.

banker's hill beer

This simple drink has saved us at many an impromptu late-night fiesta.

1	(6-ounce) can frozen limeade concentrate
1	limeade can water
1	limeade can vodka
4	(12-ounce) cans light beer, chilled

Combine the limeade concentrate, water, vodka and beer in a pitcher and mix well. Pour over ice in glasses.

Serves 6 to 8

midnight craving

This velvety smooth concoction was first created at George's at the Cove, a La Jolla landmark. Believe it or not, the traditional garnish is a pickle.

2	scoops vanilla ice cream
1	pint fresh raspberries
1/2	cup milk
	Chocolate syrup
1	pickle (optional)

Combine the ice cream, raspberries and milk in a blender and process until blended. Pour into a chilled glass and drizzle with chocolate syrup. Serve with the pickle.

Serves 1

tijuana sunrise

If you're up late enough to see it get early, you'll need this eye-opener.

2	ounces tequila
4	ounces fresh orange juice
1/2	ounce angostura bitters

Combine the tequila and orange juice in a mixing glass partially filled with ice and stir gently. Strain into a highball glass over ice. Place a spoon in the highball glass and gradually pour the bitters down the spoon, allowing to settle at the bottom of the glass.

Serves 1

red chile popcorn

A perfect late-night complement to our Banker's Hill Beer. Serve with old movies. . .*Some Like It Hot*, perhaps?

8	cups freshly popped popcorn
1/4	cup (1/2 stick) butter
2	small dried red chile peppers
1/2	teaspoon garlic salt
2	cups roasted peanuts (optional)

Preheat the oven to 200 degrees. Place the popcorn in a large baking pan and keep warm in the oven. Heat the butter in a saucepan over low heat until melted. Stir in the chile peppers. Cook for 5 minutes, stirring occasionally. Discard the chile peppers, reserving the butter. Pour the chile butter over the popcorn and toss to coat. Add the garlic salt and peanuts and toss to mix.

Serves 6 to 8

sun-dried tomato and goat cheese bruschetta

These are late-night, toasted heaven.

8   (1/4- to 3/4-inch) slices rustic Italian or French baguette
     Garlic cloves, sliced

1   plum tomato, cut into 1/4-inch pieces

2   tablespoons finely chopped drained oil-pack sun-dried tomatoes

2   tablespoons minced fresh basil

1   teaspoon extra-virgin olive oil

1/4   teaspoon freshly ground pepper, or to taste

1/8   teaspoon salt, or to taste

3   tablespoons fresh white goat cheese

3   tablespoons freshly grated Parmesan cheese

TIP   *Much of this appetizer can be prepared in advance. The bread can be toasted earlier in the day, and the tomato mixture may be prepared up to one day in advance and stored, covered, in the refrigerator. Bring to room temperature, assemble, and broil just before serving.*

Position the oven rack 4 to 5 inches from the heat source and preheat the broiler. Arrange the bread slices in a single layer on a baking sheet. Broil for 1 minute per side or until light brown, turning once. The slices should be golden brown and crisp on the outside and chewy and soft on the inside. Rub 1 side of each slice with the sliced garlic. The more you rub, the stronger the flavor.

Combine the plum tomato, sun-dried tomatoes, basil, olive oil, pepper and salt in a bowl and mix well. Spread the garlic-rubbed side of each bread slice with some of the goat cheese and top with some of the tomato mixture. Sprinkle with the Parmesan cheese. Broil for 1 1/2 minutes or until the cheese melts. Serve warm or at room temperature.

Serves 2 to 4

sun-dried tomato and goat cheese bruschetta

clam toasties

We won't hear one word against these comforting snack bites—and neither will you.

1   (6- to 7-ounce) can minced
    clams
8   ounces cream cheese, softened
1   teaspoon Worcestershire sauce
    Garlic salt to taste
    Onion powder to taste
1   baguette, thinly sliced
    Paprika to taste

TIP   *This also works as a dip with
crudités or breadsticks.*

Preheat the oven to 375 degrees. Drain the clams, reserving the liquid. Beat the cream cheese, clams, Worcestershire sauce, garlic salt and onion powder in a mixing bowl until combined. Add the reserved liquid gradually until the desired consistency and flavor and mix well.

Spread the clam mixture on 1 side of each bread slice and arrange on a baking sheet. Sprinkle with paprika. Bake for 8 to 10 minutes or until bubbly.

Serves 10

clam toasties

avocado and black bean salsa

Who says you can't be healthy and fresh at midnight?

4   plum tomatoes, finely chopped
1   (15-ounce) can black beans,
     drained and rinsed
2   avocados, finely chopped
1/2 cup finely chopped red onion
3   tablespoons lime juice
1   teaspoon chipotle sauce, or
     to taste
     Salt to taste

Combine the tomatoes, beans, avocados, onion, lime juice, chipotle sauce and salt in a bowl and mix gently. Let stand at room temperature for 30 minutes and serve with tortilla chips. You may prepare up to 3 hours in advance and store, covered, in the refrigerator. If preparing in advance, place the avocado pits in the salsa to prevent the avocados from turning brown.

Serves 10

southwestern cheesecake dip

We strongly recommend making a double batch of this dip—especially if there are a lot of hungry men present.

16 ounces cream cheese, softened
1   cup sour cream
2   eggs
2   cups (8 ounces) shredded
    Pepper Jack cheese
1   (7-ounce) can green chiles
    Chopped tomatoes
    Chopped fresh cilantro
    Chopped green onions
    Chopped avocado
    Chopped black olives

Preheat the oven to 325 degrees. Combine the cream cheese, sour cream and eggs in a mixing bowl and beat until smooth. Fold in the Pepper Jack cheese and green chiles. Spoon the cream cheese mixture into a 9-inch springform pan. Bake for 35 minutes. Cool in the pan on a wire rack. Store, covered, in the refrigerator.

Remove the side of the pan 1 hour before serving and arrange the tomatoes, cilantro, green onions, avocado and olives in a decorative pattern over the top of the cheesecake. Serve with assorted party crackers.

Serves 12 to 15

definitive macaroni and cheese

So, you'll probably have to make it sometime during the day. But we can't think of a more heart-warming midnight snack than this classic dish.

8	ounces elbow macaroni
2	cups milk
1/4	cup (1/2 stick) butter
1/4	cup flour
1	teaspoon salt
1/2	teaspoon Tabasco sauce
	Freshly ground pepper to taste
1/2	cup heavy cream
1	pound sharp Cheddar cheese, shredded

Preheat the oven to 350 degrees. Cook the pasta using the package directions. Drain and place the pasta in a large bowl. Warm the milk in a small saucepan over medium heat. Melt the butter in a saucepan over low heat. Whisk the flour into the butter and cook for 3 minutes or until smooth and bubbly, stirring constantly. Add the warm milk gradually, stirring constantly. Increase the heat to medium-high and bring the sauce just to a boil, stirring frequently. Reduce the heat to low.

Simmer for a few minutes, stirring occasionally. Stir in the salt, Tabasco sauce and pepper. Add the heavy cream and mix well. Simmer for 3 to 4 minutes, stirring occasionally. Stir in 12 ounces of the cheese and simmer until blended, stirring frequently. Pour the cheese sauce over the pasta and stir to coat. Spoon the pasta mixture into a baking pan and sprinkle with the remaining 4 ounces of cheese. Bake for 20 to 30 minutes or until bubbly. Broil if desired for 2 to 3 minutes or just until the top is brown.

Serves 4 to 6

definitive macaroni and cheese

zesty grilled cheese sandwiches

These easy-to-make sandwiches will put a little spring in your step, even if it is 2 a.m.

2   tablespoons butter
8   (1-ounce) slices bread
4   slices medium Cheddar cheese
1   large tomato, cut into 4 slices
2   serrano chiles, seeded and
     thinly sliced
1   teaspoon chopped fresh basil
     Salt and pepper to taste

Preheat a griddle or a cast-iron skillet over medium heat. Spread the butter on 1 side of each bread slice and arrange 4 of the bread slices butter side down on the hot griddle. Layer each with 1 cheese slice, 1 tomato slice, several serrano chile slices and some of the basil. Sprinkle with salt and pepper and top with the remaining bread slices butter side up.

Cook for 3 to 4 minutes or until the cheese just begins to melt and turn. Cook for 3 to 4 minutes longer. Serve immediately.

Makes 4 sandwiches

crazy strawberries with vanilla ice cream

Impress your guests with late-night culture. This is a traditional Italian dish that you will go "pazzo" for.

1 cup sliced fresh strawberries
1 cup sugar
3/4 cup water
1/4 cup balsamic vinegar
1/4 teaspoon freshly ground pepper
Vanilla ice cream
Freshly ground pepper to taste

Reserve several sliced strawberries for garnish if desired. Mix the sugar and water in a saucepan and cook over medium heat until the sugar dissolves, stirring frequently. Stir in the strawberries, vinegar and 1/4 teaspoon pepper.

Cook for 10 minutes longer or until the mixture is of a syrupy consistency, stirring occasionally. Spoon the strawberry mixture over scoops of vanilla ice cream in dessert bowls. Garnish with the reserved strawberry slices and sprinkle with freshly ground pepper to taste.

Serves 6

easy chocolate sauce

This recipe is not only easy, but it's also fast and fabulous.

1   (14-ounce) can sweetened
     condensed milk
1/4 cup (1/2 stick) butter, softened
1/4 teaspoon salt (optional)
1   cup (6 ounces) semisweet
     chocolate chips
1   teaspoon vanilla extract
1/3 to 1/2 cup coffee liqueur,
     brandy or strong coffee

TIP   *This sauce stores well in an
airtight jar in the refrigerator and can
be spooned out and heated up as
needed—or just eaten off the spoon.*

Combine the condensed milk, butter and salt in a microwave-safe bowl. Microwave for 3 to 3 1/2 minutes or until the mixture comes to a boil, stirring halfway through. Stir and microwave for 45 seconds longer. Add the chocolate chips and vanilla and stir until blended. Blend in the liqueur and ladle over your favorite dessert.

Makes about 2 1/4 cups

one-pan chocolate cake

This is so good—chocolately, fudgy, and fun—that we know it'll become a kitchen staple.

CAKE

1	(16-ounce) can chocolate syrup
1	cup sifted flour
3/4	cup sugar
1/2	cup (1 stick) unsalted butter, softened
4	eggs
2	teaspoons baking powder
1	teaspoon vanilla extract
1/16	teaspoon salt

FUDGE FROSTING

2	ounces unsweetened chocolate
1	(14-ounce) can sweetened condensed milk
1/8	teaspoon salt
1	tablespoon cold water

TIP   *We love to enjoy this on the Fourth of July after the fireworks with a cold glass of milk.*

CAKE   Preheat the oven to 325 degrees. Combine the syrup, flour, sugar, butter, eggs, baking powder, vanilla and salt in a mixing bowl and beat until blended. Spoon the batter into a buttered 8×8-inch cake pan. Bake for 40 minutes or until the center springs back when lightly touched. Cool in the pan on a wire rack.

FROSTING   Combine the chocolate, condensed milk and salt in a double boiler. Cook over simmering water until thick and smooth, stirring frequently. Remove from the heat and stir in the cold water. Spread the frosting over the top of the cake.

Serves 8

indoor s'mores

Bring this childhood classic in from the campground.

1   cup (2 sticks) butter, melted
3   cups graham cracker crumbs
1/3   cup sugar
2   cups (12 ounces) chocolate
      chips
3   cups miniature marshmallows

Preheat the oven to 350 degrees. Brush a 9×13-inch baking dish with some of the melted butter. Combine the remaining melted butter, cracker crumbs and sugar in a bowl and mix well.

Pat 1/2 of the crumb mixture over the bottom of the prepared baking dish. Sprinkle with the chocolate chips and marshmallows. Top with the remaining crumb mixture and flatten with a spatula. Bake for 10 minutes or until the marshmallows melt. Cool for 5 minutes before cutting into squares.

Makes 2 to 3 dozen s'mores

iced chunky pumpkin cookies

These are so yummy, you'll make them any old time—but they also provide some valuable late-night nutrition.

COOKIES

1 cup (2 sticks) butter

1/2 cup packed brown sugar

1/2 cup sugar

1 1/2 teaspoons cinnamon

1 teaspoon ginger

1 teaspoon baking powder

1/2 teaspoon baking soda

1/2 teaspoon salt

1/2 teaspoon nutmeg

1/4 teaspoon ground cloves

1 cup puréed cooked pumpkin or canned pumpkin

1 egg

1 cup whole wheat flour or all-purpose flour

1 cup all-purpose flour or whole wheat flour

1 cup granola or rolled oats

1 cup chopped walnuts, cashews or almonds

1 cup (6 ounces) white chocolate chips

1 cup dried cranberries

CONFECTIONERS' SUGAR ICING

2 cups confectioners' sugar

1/4 cup (1/2 stick) butter, softened

3 tablespoons milk or cream

COOKIES   Preheat the oven to 350 degrees. Beat the butter, brown sugar and sugar in a mixing bowl until creamy, scraping the bowl occasionally. Add the cinnamon, ginger, baking powder, baking soda, salt, nutmeg and cloves and beat until blended. Beat in the pumpkin and egg. Add the whole wheat flour and all-purpose flour and beat until smooth. Stir in the granola, walnuts, chocolate chips and cranberries.

Drop the dough onto a nonstick cookie sheet using an ice cream scoop or spoon. Bake for 15 to 18 minutes or until golden brown. Cool on the cookie sheet for 2 minutes. Remove to a wire rack to cool completely. You may add 1 cup shredded coconut and/or 1 cup golden raisins.

ICING   Combine the confectioners' sugar, butter and milk in a mixing bowl and beat until of a spreading consistency, scraping the bowl occasionally. Spread the icing over the tops of the cooled cookies.

Makes 2 dozen cookies

glossary of cooking techniques

bake . . . . To cook by dry heat in an oven or under hot coals.

bard . . . . To cover lean meats with bacon or pork fat before cooking to prevent dryness.

baste . . . . . . To moisten, especially meats, with melted butter, pan drippings, sauce, etc., during cooking time.

beat . . . . To mix ingredients by vigorous stirring or with an electric mixer.

blanch . . . . . To immerse, usually vegetables or fruit, briefly into boiling water to inactivate enzymes, loosen skin, or soak away excess salt.

blend . . . . . . To combine two or more ingredients, at least one of which is liquid or soft, to quickly produce a mixture that has a smooth, uniform consistency.

boil . . . . To heat liquid until bubbly; the boiling point for water is about 212 degrees, depending on the altitude and the atmospheric pressure.

braise . . . . . . To cook, especially meats, covered, in a small amount of liquid.

brew . . . . . . To prepare a beverage by allowing boiling water to extract flavor and/or color from certain substances.

broil . . . . To cook by direct exposure to intense heat such as a flame or an electric heating unit.

caramelize . . To melt sugar in a heavy pan over low heat until golden brown, stirring constantly.

chill . . . . To cool in the refrigerator or in cracked ice.

clarify . . . . . To remove impurities from melted butter or margarine by allowing the sediment to settle, then pouring off clear yellow liquid. Other fats may be clarified by straining.

cream . . . . . . To blend shortening, butter, or margarine, which usually has been softened, or sometimes oil, with a granulated or crushed ingredient until the mixture is soft and creamy. Usually described in method as light and fluffy.

curdle . . . . . . To congeal milk with rennet or heat until solid lumps or curds are formed.

cut in . . . . . . To disperse solid shortening into dry ingredients with a knife or pastry blender. Texture of the mixture should resemble coarse cracker meal. Described in method as crumbly.

decant . . . . . To pour a liquid such as wine or melted butter carefully from one container into another, leaving the sediment in the original container.

deep-fry . . . . To cook in a deep pan or skillet containing hot cooking oil. Deep-fried foods are generally completely immersed in the hot oil.

deglaze . . . . To heat stock, wine, or other liquid in the pan in which meat has been cooked, mixing with pan juices and sediment to form a gravy or sauce base.

degorge . . . . To remove strong flavors or impurities before cooking, i.e., soaking ham in cold water or sprinkling vegetables with salt, then letting stand for a period of time and pressing out excess fluid.

glossary of cooking techniques

degrease . . . To remove accumulated fat from surface of hot liquids.

dice . . . . To cut into small cubes about 1/4 inch in size. Do not use dice unless ingredient can truly be cut into cubes.

dissolve . . . . To create a solution by thoroughly mixing a solid or granular substance with a liquid until no sediment remains.

dredge . . . . . To coat completely with flour, bread crumbs, etc.

fillet . . . . To remove bones from meat or fish. (Pieces of meat, fish, or poultry from which bones have been removed are called fillets.)

flambé . . . . . To pour warmed brandy or other spirits over food in a pan, then ignite and continue cooking briefly.

fold in . . . . . To blend a delicate frothy mixture into a heavier one so that none of the lightness or volume is lost. Using a rubber spatula, turn under and bring up and over, rotating bowl 1/4 turn after each folding motion.

fry . . . . To cook in a pan or skillet containing hot cooking oil. The oil should not totally cover the food.

garnish . . . . . To decorate food before serving.

glaze . . . . . . To cover or coat with sauce, syrup, egg white, or a jellied substance. After applying, it becomes firm, adding color and flavor.

grate . . . . . . To rub food against a rough, perforated utensil to produce slivers, chunks, curls, etc.

gratiné . . . . . To top a sauced dish with crumbs, cheese, or butter, then brown under a broiler.

grill . . . . To broil, usually over hot coals or charcoal.

grind . . . . . . To cut, crush, or force through a chopper to produce small bits.

infuse . . . . . . To steep herbs or other flavorings in a liquid until liquid absorbs flavor.

julienne . . . . To cut vegetables, fruit, etc., into long thin strips.

knead . . . . . To press, fold, and stretch dough until smooth and elastic. Method usually notes time frame or result.

lard . . . . To insert strips of fat or bacon into lean meat to keep it moist and juicy during cooking. Larding is an internal basting technique.

leaven . . . . . To cause batters and doughs to rise, usually by means of a chemical leavening agent. This process may occur before or during baking.

marinate . . . To soak, usually in a highly seasoned oil-acid solution, to flavor and/or tenderize food.

melt . . . . To liquefy solid foods by the action of heat.

mince . . . . . . To cut or chop into very small pieces.

glossary of cooking techniques

mix. . . . . To combine ingredients to distribute uniformly.

mold. . . . . . . To shape into a particular form.

panbroil. . . . To cook in a skillet or pan using a very small amount of fat to prevent sticking.

panfry. . . . . To cook in a skillet or pan containing only a small amount of fat.

parboil. . . . . To partially cook in boiling water. Most parboiled foods require additional cooking with or without other ingredients.

parch. . . . . . To dry or roast slightly through exposure to intense heat.

pit. . . . . To remove the hard inedible seed from peaches, plums, etc.

plank. . . . . . To broil and serve on a board or wooden platter.

plump. . . . . To soak fruits, usually dried, in liquid until puffy and softened.

poach. . . . . . To cook in a small amount of gently simmering liquid.

preserve. . . . To prevent food spoilage by pickling, salting, dehydration, smoking, boiling in syrup, etc. Preserved foods have excellent keeping qualities when properly prepared and stored.

purée. . . . . . To reduce the pulp of cooked fruit and vegetables to a smooth and thick liquid by straining or blending.

reduce. . . . . To boil stock, gravy, or other liquid until volume is reduced, liquid is thickened, and flavor is intensified.

refresh. . . . . To place blanched drained vegetables or other food in cold water to halt cooking process.

render. . . . . To cook meat or meat trimmings at low temperature until fat melts and can be drained and strained.

roast. . . . . . (1) To cook by dry heat either in an oven or over hot coals. (2) To dry or parch by intense heat.

sauté. . . . . . To cook quickly in a skillet containing a small amount of hot cooking oil. Sautéed foods should never be immersed in the cooking oil and should be stirred frequently.

scald. . . . . . (1) To heat a liquid almost to the boiling point. (2) To soak, usually vegetables or fruit, in boiling water until the skins are loosened; see blanch, which is our preferred term for (2).

scallop. . . . . To bake with a sauce in a casserole. The food may either be mixed or layered with the sauce.

score. . . . . . To make shallow cuts diagonally in parallel lines, especially in meat.

glossary of cooking techniques

scramble . . . To cook and stir simultaneously, especially eggs.

shirr . . . . To crack eggs into individual buttered baking dishes, then bake or broil until whites are set. Chopped meats or vegetables, cheese, cream, or bread crumbs may also be added.

shred . . . . . . To cut or shave food into slivers.

shuck . . . . . . To remove the husk from corn or the shell from oysters, clams, etc.

sieve . . . . To press a mixture through a closely meshed metal utensil to make it homogenous.

sift . . . . To pass, usually dry ingredients, through a fine wire mesh in order to produce a uniform consistency.

simmer . . . . . To cook in or with a liquid at just below the boiling point.

skewer . . . . . (1) To thread, usually meat and vegetables, onto a sharpened rod (as in shish kabob). (2) To fasten the opening of stuffed fowl closed with small pins.

skim . . . . To ladle or spoon off excess fat or scum from the surface of a liquid.

smoke . . . . . To preserve or cook through continuous exposure to wood smoke for a long time.

steam . . . . . . To cook with water vapor in a closed container, usually in a steamer, on a rack, or in a double boiler.

sterilize . . . . To cleanse and purify through exposure to intense heat.

stew . . . . To simmer, usually meats and vegetables, for a long period of time. Also used to tenderize meats.

stir-fry . . . . . To cook small pieces of vegetables and/or meat in a small amount of oil in a wok or skillet over high heat until tender-crisp, stirring constantly.

strain . . . . . . To pass through a strainer, sieve, or cheesecloth to break down or remove solids or impurities.

stuff . . . . To fill or pack cavities, especially those of meats, vegetables, and poultry.

toast . . . . To brown and crisp, usually by means of direct heat, or to bake until brown.

toss . . . . To mix lightly with a lifting motion using two forks or spoons.

truss . . . . To bind poultry legs and wings close to the body before cooking.

whip . . . . To beat a mixture until air has been thoroughly incorporated and the mixture is light and fluffy, the volume is greatly increased, and the mixture holds its shape.

wilt . . . . To apply heat to cause dehydration, or color change, and a droopy appearance.

equivalents

when the recipe calls for . . . . use

baking

1/2 cup butter. . . . . 4 ounces
2 cups butter. . . . . 1 pound
4 cups all-purpose flour. . . . . 1 pound
4 1/2 to 5 cups sifted cake flour . . . . 1 pound
1 square chocolate . . . . 1 ounce
1 cup semisweet chocolate chips . . . . 6 ounces
4 cups marshmallows. . . . . 1 pound
2 1/4 cups packed brown sugar . . . . 1 pound
4 cups confectioners' sugar. . . . . 1 pound
2 cups granulated sugar . . . . 1 pound

cereal/bread

1 cup fine dry bread crumbs . . . . 4 to 5 slices
1 cup soft bread crumbs. . . . . 2 slices
1 cup small bread cubes. . . . . 2 slices
1 cup fine cracker crumbs. 28 saltines
1 cup fine graham cracker crumbs . . . . 15 crackers
1 cup vanilla wafer crumbs . . . . 22 wafers
1 cup crushed cornflakes . . . . 3 cups uncrushed
4 cups cooked macaroni. 8 ounces uncooked
3 1/2 cups cooked rice . . . . 1 cup uncooked

dairy

1 cup shredded cheese. . . . . 4 ounces
1 cup cottage cheese . . . . 8 ounces
1 cup sour cream . . . . 8 ounces
1 cup whipped cream . . . . 1/2 cup heavy cream
2/3 cup evaporated milk. . . . . 1 small can
1 2/3 cups evaporated milk . . . . 1 (13-ounce) can

fruit

4 cups sliced or chopped apples . . . . 4 medium
1 cup mashed bananas . . . . 3 medium
2 cups pitted cherries. . . . . 4 cups unpitted

equivalents

when the recipe calls for . . . . use

fruit (continued)
2¹/₂ cups shredded coconut. . . . . 8 ounces
4 cups cranberries . . . . 1 pound
1 cup pitted dates. . . . . 1 (8-ounce) package
1 cup candied fruit . . . . 1 (8-ounce) package
3 to 4 tablespoons lemon juice plus
1 tablespoon grated lemon rind . . . . 1 lemon
¹/₃ cup orange juice plus
2 teaspoons grated orange rind . . . . 1 orange
4 cups sliced peaches . . . . 8 medium
2 cups pitted prunes . . . . 1 (12-ounce) package
3 cups raisins . . . . 1 (15-ounce) package

meats
4 cups chopped cooked chicken . . . . 1 (5-pound) chicken
3 cups chopped cooked meat. . . . . 1 pound, cooked
2 cups cooked ground meat. . . . . 1 pound, cooked

nuts
1 cup chopped nuts . . . . 4 ounces shelled or
1 pound unshelled

vegetables
2 cups cooked green beans . . . . ¹/₂ pound fresh or
1 (16-ounce) can
2¹/₂ cups lima beans or red beans . . . . 1 cup dried, cooked
4 cups shredded cabbage . . . . 1 pound
1 cup grated carrot. . . . . 1 large
8 ounces fresh mushrooms . . . . 1 (4-ounce) can
1 cup chopped onion . . . . 1 large
4 cups sliced or chopped potatoes . . . . 4 medium
2 cups canned tomatoes . . . . 1 (16-ounce) can

measurement equivalents

3 teaspoons	1 tablespoon
2 tablespoons	$1/8$ cup
4 tablespoons	$1/4$ cup
5 tablespoons plus 1 teaspoon	$1/3$ cup
8 tablespoons	$1/2$ cup
12 tablespoons	$3/4$ cup
16 tablespoons	1 cup
32 tablespoons	2 cups
64 tablespoons	1 quart
96 tablespoons	$1 1/2$ quarts
1 ounce	2 tablespoons fat or liquid
4 ounces	$1/2$ cup
8 ounces	1 cup
16 ounces	1 pound
$5/8$ cup	$1/2$ cup plus 2 tablespoons equals 10 tablespoons
$7/8$ cup	$3/4$ cup plus 2 tablespoons equals 14 tablespoons
2 cups	1 pint
2 pints	1 quart
1 quart	4 cups
4 quarts	1 gallon

container measurements

can size	weight	approximate cups
8 ounces	8 ounces	1
Picnic	$10 1/2$ to 12 ounces	$1 1/4$
12 ounces vacuum	12 ounces	$1 1/2$
No. 300	14 to 16 ounces	$1 3/4$
No. 303	16 to 17 ounces	2
No. 2	20 ounces	$2 1/2$
No. $2 1/2$	28 to 29 ounces	$3 1/2$
Baby foods	4 to 8 ounces	
Condensed milk	14 ounces	$1 1/3$
Evaporated milk	5 ounces or 12 ounces	$2/3$ or $1 2/3$

metric equivalents

These metric measures are approximate benchmarks for purposes of home food preparation. 1 milliliter = 1 cubic centimeter = 1 gram

liquid
1 teaspoon = 5 milliliters
1 tablespoon = 15 milliliters
1 fluid ounce = 30 milliliters
1 cup = 250 milliliters
1 pint = 500 milliliters

dry
1 quart = 1 liter
1 ounce = 30 grams
1 pound = 450 grams
2.2 pounds = 1 kilogram

weight
1 ounce = 28 grams
1 pound = 450 grams

length
1 inch = $2^1/_2$ centimeters
$^1/_{16}$ inch = 1 millimeter

formulas using conversion factors

When approximate conversions are not accurate enough, use these formulas to convert measures from one system to another.

measurements
ounces to grams
grams to ounces
pounds to grams
pounds to kilograms
ounces to milliliters
cups to liters
inches to centimeters
centimeters to inches

formulas
ounces × 28.3 = # grams
grams × 0.035 = # ounces
pounds × 453.6 = # grams
pounds × 0.45 = # kilograms
ounces × 30 = # milliliters
cups × 0.24 = # liters
inches × 2.54 = # centimeters
centimeters × 0.39 = # inches

basic substitutions

if the recipe calls for **you can substitute**

flour

1 cup sifted all-purpose flour . . . . 1 cup less 2 tablespoons unsifted all-purpose flour

1 cup sifted cake flour . . . . 1 cup less 2 tablespoons sifted all-purpose flour

1 cup sifted self-rising flour . . . . 1 cup sifted all-purpose flour plus 1^1/2 teaspoons baking powder and a pinch of salt

milk/cream

1 cup buttermilk . . . . 1 cup plain yogurt, or 1 tablespoon lemon juice or vinegar plus enough milk to measure 1 cup—let stand for 5 minutes before using

1 cup whipping cream or half-and-half . . . . 7/8 cup whole milk plus 1^1/2 tablespoons butter

1 cup light cream . . . . 7/8 cup whole milk plus 3 tablespoons butter

1 cup sour cream . . . . 1 cup plain yogurt

1 cup sour milk. . . . . 1 cup plain yogurt

1 cup whole milk . . . . 1 cup skim or nonfat milk plus 2 tablespoons butter or margarine

seasonings

1 teaspoon allspice . . . . 1/2 teaspoon cinnamon plus 1/8 teaspoon cloves

1 cup ketchup. . . . . 1 cup tomato sauce plus 1/2 cup sugar plus 2 tablespoons vinegar

1 teaspoon Italian spice . . . . 1/4 teaspoon each oregano, basil, thyme, and rosemary plus dash of cayenne pepper

1 teaspoon lemon juice . . . . 1/2 teaspoon vinegar

basic substitutions

sugar

1 cup confectioners' sugar	$^1/_2$ cup plus 1 tablespoon granulated sugar
1 cup granulated sugar	$1^3/_4$ cups confectioners' sugar, 1 cup packed light brown sugar, or $^3/_4$ cup honey

other

1 package active dry yeast	$^1/_2$ cake compressed yeast
1 teaspoon baking powder	$^1/_4$ teaspoon cream of tartar plus $^1/_4$ teaspoon baking soda
1 cup dry bread crumbs	$^3/_4$ cup cracker crumbs or 1 cup cornflake crumbs
1 cup (2 sticks) butter	$^7/_8$ cup vegetable oil or 1 cup margarine
1 tablespoon cornstarch	2 tablespoons all-purpose flour
1 cup dark corn syrup	$^3/_4$ cup light corn syrup plus $^1/_4$ cup light molasses
1 cup light corn syrup	1 cup maple syrup
$1^2/_3$ ounces semisweet chocolate	1 ounce unsweetened chocolate plus 4 teaspoons granulated sugar
1 ounce unsweetened chocolate	3 tablespoons unsweetened baking cocoa plus 1 tablespoon butter or margarine
1 (1-ounce) square chocolate	$^1/_4$ cup baking cocoa plus 1 teaspoon shortening
1 cup honey	1 to $1^1/_4$ cups sugar plus $^1/_4$ cup liquid, or 1 cup corn syrup or molasses
currants	raisins
1 egg	$^1/_4$ cup mayonnaise

baking dishes

if you don't have	try using
1-quart baking dish	.9-inch pie plate
	8-inch round or square cake pan
	4×7-inch loaf pan
1½-quart baking dish	.10-inch pie plate
	9-inch round or square cake pan
	4×8-inch loaf pan
2-quart baking dish	.7×11-inch baking dish
	5×9-inch loaf pan
2½-quart baking dish	.8×12-inch baking dish
	10×15-inch jelly roll pan
3-quart baking dish	.9×13-inch baking pan

volume of special baking pans

7½-inch tube pan	6 cups
9-inch tube pan	9 to 12 cups
10-inch tube pan	12 to 16 cups
8-inch springform pan	12 cups
9-inch springform pan	16 cups
8-inch ring mold	4 cups
9-inch ring mold	8 cups

Remember that if it is necessary to divide the recipe between smaller pans, the baking times must be adjusted to allow for the reduced volume of each pan. When using glass baking dishes, the oven temperature should usually be reduced by 25 degrees.

Pans with nonstick coatings such as Teflon and ironstone may need special handling. The finish will be more durable if washed by hand instead of in the dishwasher. When the contents must be turned out of the pan (such as a cake), the pans should be greased and floured in the usual manner.

servings or yields

appetizers . . . . Appetizers are tricky and can either be estimated by the number of servings or number of people served. You can estimate the number of people you would serve with the recipe, assuming everyone eats about the same amount. You can also estimate the volume of a dip in tablespoons or the number of pieces made and consider each one a serving.

beverages . . . . Tall drinks usually yield about 8 ounces per serving; punch usually yields about 4 ounces per serving.

breads . . . . A loaf of bread is estimated to yield 12 slices; each one is a serving. For biscuits and rolls, the guideline is the number of cups of flour: 2 cups of flour will yield about 12 biscuits or rolls, and each biscuit or roll is a serving. An 8- or 9-inch pan will serve 9.

cakes . . . . Base your estimate on the size of the pan. A 9×13-inch pan will yield 15 servings. An 8- or 9-inch layer cake will yield 12 to 16 servings. A tube or bundt pan will yield 16 servings. Cake rolls will serve 8 to 12.

cookies . . . . Use the number of cups of flour: 2 cups will yield 2 dozen cookies. Take into account, however, the number of add-ins and whether the dough is to be shaped or dropped.

candies . . . . Estimate the number of pieces it will make, and call each one a serving.

casseroles and desserts . . . . Estimate 6 to 8 servings from a 2-quart dish and 10 from a 3-quart or 9×13-inch dish. Softer desserts yield $1/2$ to $3/4$ cup per serving, depending on the richness of the dessert.

main dishes . . . . Most meats, chicken, and seafood will yield 1 serving from 4 to 6 ounces of uncooked boneless meat. Use the casserole estimate for main dish casseroles, or estimate 1 to $1 1/2$ cups per serving.

pies . . . . Pies will serve 6 to 8, depending on whether they are deep-dish or rich.

salads . . . . Estimate or measure the total volume of the ingredients and allow $3/4$ to 1 cup per serving for heavy or sweet salads and up to 2 cups for tossed salads or main dish salads.

vegetables . . . . Most vegetables and side dishes are adequate with $1/2$-cup servings, but rich or starchy dishes may be less, and light vegetables may need larger servings.

Many factors should be taken into account when determining the yield of a recipe. These include the appetite of the diners, the number of courses to be served, as well as the age and sex of the guests.

index

index

index

index

index

index

CALIFORNIA sol food

CASUAL COOKING FROM THE JUNIOR LEAGUE OF SAN DIEGO

Junior League of San Diego
210 Maple Street
San Diego, California 92103

Name

_____

Street Address

_____

City   State   Zip

_____

Telephone

YOUR ORDER	QUANTITY	TOTAL
California Sol Food at $29.95 per book		$
Postage and handling at $4.00 per book		$
California residents add 7.75% sales tax		$
TOTAL		$

Method of Payment: [   ] MasterCard   [   ] VISA

[   ] Check enclosed payable to Junior League of San Diego

_____

Account Number   Expiration Date

_____

Signature

To order, return this form with your check or credit card information to
JLSD, 210 Maple Street, San Diego, CA 92103,
or visit www.californiasolfood.com and buy online.

Photocopies accepted.